THE WAY OF KINSHIP

THE WAY OF KINSHIP

An Anthology of
Native Siberian Literature

TRANSLATED AND EDITED BY
ALEXANDER VASCHENKO AND CLAUDE CLAYTON SMITH

FOREWORD BY N. SCOTT MOMADAY

FIRST PEOPLES
New Directions in Indigenous Studies

University of Minnesota Press
MINNEAPOLIS • LONDON

The Way of Kinship was first published as a special issue of *North Dakota Quarterly* 69, no. 3 (2003). This expanded edition adds writing by Vladimir Sangi, Maria Vagatova, and Yuri Rytkheu; artwork by Gennady Raishev; and additions to original selections by Yeremei Aipin.

The poems "My Word, My Tongue" and "Dirge for the Land of the Khanty" by Maria Vagatova, and "Evenk Invocations for Good Fortune" were published in Robert Hedin, ed., *Great River Review* 47 (2000): 1–4.

The poem "To the Bear" by Yuri Vaella was published in C. B. Follett, ed., *Grrrrr: A Collection of Poems about Bears* (Sausalito: Arctos Press, 2000), 129.

The map of Siberia was created by Harry J. Wilson, geographer, in consultation with Susan Scarberry-García, visiting scholar, Department of English, University of New Mexico.

Published by the University of Minnesota Press
111 Third Avenue South, Suite 290
Minneapolis, MN 55401-2520
http://www.upress.umn.edu

Library of Congress Cataloging-in-Publication Data

The way of kinship : an anthology of native Siberian literature / translated and edited by Alexander Vaschenko and Claude Clayton Smith ; foreword by N. Scott Momaday.
    p. cm. — (First peoples: new directions in indigenous studies)
    Includes bibliographical references.
    ISBN 978-0-8166-7080-2 (hc : alk. paper) — ISBN 978-0-8166-7081-9 (pbk. : alk. paper)
    1. Siberia (Russia)—Literary collections.   2. Ethnic groups—Russia (Federation)—Siberia—Literary collections.   3. Russian literature—Russia (Federation)—Siberia—Translations into English.   I. Vaschenko, A. (Aleksandr).   II. Smith, Claude Clayton, 1944–.
    PG3213.W39 2010
    808.8'9957—dc22   2010035079

Printed in the United States of America on acid-free paper

The University of Minnesota is an equal-opportunity educator and employer.

17 16 15 14 13 12 11 10   10 9 8 7 6 5 4 3 2 1

To native storytellers, old and new

contents

(

Foreword

(

N. Scott Momaday

Once, at a remote reindeer camp in western Siberia, I saw the skull of a bear fixed to a tree. In the writings of my friend Yeremei Aipin, I had read of the Khanty Bear Feast, a sacred ceremony that celebrates the ancient spiritual relationship between man and bear. Still later, at the opening of a writers' union headquartered in Khanty-Mansiisk, I ate the heart of a bear without knowing it. It was a delicacy, prepared on open flames and served on skewers. When I discovered what I had eaten, I was disturbed, for my people, the Kiowas of the Southern Great Plains of the United States, do not eat bear meat. It is a taboo and thought of as cannibalism. But on reflection I came to see that my heart and the heart of the bear had been conjoined in a special way as a matter not of coincidence but of fate. My Indian name, *Tsoai-talee,* comes from a story about a boy who turns into a bear. In Siberia, at every turn I found ancient bonds of kinship, common denominators that are indispensable integrations of the indigenous world.

In the Khanty Bear ceremony, one of the principal participants is a singer. He carries a stick on which there are a hundred notches. Each notch represents a song. The singer sings these hundred songs during the ceremony, which lasts four or five days. The songs are committed to the singer's memory. This is a remarkable feat of memorization and indicates beyond doubt that the oral tradition of the Khanty people is as vital as was the oral tradition of the Anglo-Saxons who recited *Beo-wulf* in the ninth century or of the Navajo singer who sings the Night

Chant in the twenty-first century. Words are the keys, language is the repository, of culture.

There is an equation that relates land to language, or language to land. The equation is sacred. As my friend Susan Scarberry-García has written (and she, too, is a student and good friend of the indigenous people of western Siberia), "Where words touch the earth, there is the sacred." What we have in this remarkable anthology is that equation realized.

The landscape of western Siberia is vast, essentially unknown to outsiders, and unforgiving. It is wilderness in the true sense. In America we have all but given up our experience, our concept, and our primordial love of wilderness. The real wilderness of the earth is diminishing at a rate almost impossible to imagine. As a result, the culture of indigenous people is being diminished in proportion. Native peoples around the world are being robbed of their sacred heritage.

I believe that this collection of writing is a repository of the native culture. Words have always been the last bastion of cultural survival. We would not have the precious literature of the Anglo-Saxons without the dedicated work of the monastic scribes. We would not have the sacred texts of the Mayan and Aztec cultures, those that have survived, without the codices that have come down through the generations of unknowing. That some of these treasures are available to us as writing is a miracle. But writing is a recent invention: the oral tradition is inestimably older.

The writings here, while altogether modern in one sense, are based on a literature, albeit oral, that has existed for thousands of years. They are the reflections of people who have lived long on the earth, on their own terms, in harmony with the powers of nature. They are invaluable to us who have so much to learn from them. These stories, poems, and songs give us a way, a sacred way, into a world that we ought to know for its own sake. It is our own world, after all.

Siberia (2010)

Introduction

CRY OF THE WILD CRANE:
THE CALL OF FORGOTTEN KINSHIP

(

Alexander Vaschenko

The emergence of Native literatures around the globe during the second half of the twentieth century is by now a
well-established cultural fact. One example of this fact is the development of Native literatures in Siberia, a striking phenomenon that requires a new set of metaphors and definitions to
describe. One such metaphor, coming from real-life experience,
seems particularly appropriate: in 1995, at the first convention
of reindeer-breeding ethnic peoples of Russia, a young Native
girl, a delegate from the Far North, brought the attention of
the audience to the urgent cultural and economic claims of her
people when she exclaimed, "Please, listen to my words as to
the cry of the wild crane!"

The comparison was striking, because it made me realize
that in order to respond to this Native speaker we must be familiar with the habits of the wild crane. Had I ever heard one?
I couldn't remember. Had anyone in the audience ever seen
a wild crane—or a reindeer, for that matter? We are vaguely
aware that these are endangered species, and for the majority
of us it quite often ends there. How are we to understand the
needs and values of those people whose daily lives *consist of* and
depend on contact with their brothers, the reindeer, and their
clan totems, the wild cranes?

Native literatures, no matter where they originate, belong

to the same endangered domain. They are of the environment, part and parcel of the primordial family to which many of the children of contemporary civilization no longer belong. Once estranged from this kinship, we the children become orphans. No wonder, then, that these ethnic literatures are often silenced, forgotten by the media, misinterpreted, or limited to a narrow readership because the public is ignorant of, and alien to, their voices. Yet behind every Native literature looms a tradition— the true hero of the stories these ethnic writers tell, traditions increasingly alienated in the postcolonial era.

It is not by chance that the second half of the twentieth century marked the beginning of an era of ethnicity, a cultural factor of world importance on all levels, including literature and visual arts, in places as disparate as Africa, Latin America, the Pacific, and . . . Siberia. Beginning in the 1960s, the United States discovered its own Native literature as the voices of Native American writers such as N. Scott Momaday, Leslie Marmon Silko, Gerald Vizenor, Maurice Kenny, Simon Ortiz, and many others introduced a new universe of ideas, imagery, and alternative values coming from the traditional cultures that abide by them.

Both insistently and eloquently, these writers spoke about the importance of communal ideals; the sacredness of the earth as our mutual home; the unity with all living creatures; the importance of the oral word, Native myth, and magic as power. Simultaneously, a similar process was under way in Russia in the territory loosely referred to as Siberia, that vast expanse between the Ural Mountains and the Pacific coast of Asia, the land of the taiga forest, mighty rivers, and mountain ranges. From time immemorial, this area has been populated by many ethnic groups large and small that migrate seasonally in varying directions, warring and trading, surviving in a harsh environment. These peoples belonged, in large part, to one of three dominant linguistic families: the Altai (such as the Evenks and the Udegeh), the

Ural-Yukagir family (the Samodian group, such as the Nenets, or the Finno-Ugric group, such as the Khanty), and the Chukchee-Kamchatka family (such as Chukchee). Economically, they were hunters, reindeer breeders (especially in the Far North), and fishermen. Migrating through their ancestral territories, they established stable routes and patterns, and they survived by living in small families and scattered clans.

Spiritually, these people either believed in a supreme sky-being who established the world, or in two brother-gods, one of whom reigned supreme above while the other, who had quarreled with him, eventually came to rule the underworld. Beneath these two brothers existed a complex hierarchy of spirits closely related to the immediate surroundings. It is easy to find many parallels to these beliefs in Native American mythology. In Siberia, too, in many Creation stories the Loon is the Earth-diver, while the Raven is an important trickster hero, especially among the peoples of the Far Northeast. Shamans, like Native American medicine men, were powerful personalities who for healing purposes could transcend the many upper and lower worlds, fighting for the endangered souls of their patients. They worked hard to protect their clans, foretell good hunting, or forecast the weather.

Twenty-eight ethnic groups now exist in the territory of Russia, whose recent history reflects the ongoing conflict between traditional culture and modern industrialized society. Russians first moved to Siberia in the seventeenth century, at the time of the famous Cossack expedition led by Yermak Timofeyevich. The Cossacks, or peasant-soldiers, were trying to progress as far inland as possible, claiming the land on behalf of the czar, who had not sent the expedition directly but encouraged the venture. Historically speaking, the Russian conquest of Siberia has never been extremely violent. Yermak warred less against local Native tribes than with the princes of the Golden Horde of Mongol invaders, who by then were well established in Siberia.

Subsequently, the czars of Russia, as they encroached on Siberia, were mainly interested in establishing a steady system of *yasak,* or tribute, paid in furs and local produce, in exchange for guns and other objects of immediate need. In this way, the Russian colonization of Siberia somewhat resembles the French colonization of North America. Certainly, Christianity (in this case, Russian Orthodoxy as the historical state religion in Russia) contributed a good deal to the strengthening of imperial ties, but Russian Orthodox missionaries by and large failed to extinguish the foundations of traditional beliefs among the Native peoples. With the passing of time, the Siberian Natives and the Russians established close relationships. The Russian monarchy even developed for the Natives their own system of government, ruled by Native elders and "princes" of the local nobility, a situation that continued for two centuries.

At the beginning of the twentieth century, as Soviet power took hold, serious changes occurred. The new regime proclaimed equality as the main principle of life—material, social, and cultural—and advocated a communal way of living. Simultaneously, it established a strong hierarchical structure of bureaucratic statesmanship. In enforcing the new ideology, the policy practitioners and executors of the party line often went to the extreme, committing grave mistakes. Under the new ethnic policy, the Native peoples of the taiga and tundra—a large part of the Siberian population—were brought under one and the same standard, regardless of the cultural differences among them. This policy, which basically ignored the Native economy and culture, had both positive and negative outcomes. Through the push toward free education and universal literacy, startling results were quickly achieved, and minimal yet necessary technology (such as radio, medical assistance, and cheap transportation) was made available to all, from the metropolis to the tundra. For the Native ethnic groups of the Far North, however, education meant a controversial system of boarding schools, usually situated far from the traditional home environment. Russian language and culture were greatly encouraged, and industrialization, a high priority, was regarded supreme. Traditional cultural practices, especially shamanism, were proclaimed outmoded and were to be discarded, often officially prohibited.

By the middle of the twentieth century, traditional Native lands had been given over to oil-drilling stations and gas pipelines, collective farms (erroneously modeled on Russian peasantry practices), and other ventures of modern industrialized society. The slogan "Soviet peoples are one family," however attractive it may sound, in practice meant the eventual assimilation of Native peoples. Yet the sense of a close neighbor relationship and mutual destiny between Native Siberians and the people of Russia developed naturally and was further strengthened by struggles with shared enemies during World War II.

Native Siberian writing resulted from this controversial, intense, and at times violent period. In order to understand it more fully, one has to remember that, like Native American writing, Native Siberian literature has always been deeply rooted in an oral tradition. Native Siberians traditionally did not develop a written language, yet they enjoyed an extremely rich heritage of storytelling, from Creation myths to fairy tales and humorous animal stories. They educated their children by means of proverbs and puzzles. Their oral poetry included a universe of songs from improvised lyrics and personal dream songs to long heroic epics, sometimes sung to the accompaniment of folk instruments such as the Khanty *ning-yuch*, a Native version of the violin.

Unfortunately, during the twentieth century, with its technological and progressivist aspirations, both the milieu and taste for this rich heritage were gradually abandoned. In Soviet times traditional spirituality and lore were not encouraged as viable subject matter or aesthetic modes for the emerging ethnic writer, who after all was not supposed to look back into the patriarchal, "primitive" past but, rather, to embrace and proclaim the bright industrial communal paradise of the future. Too often the digressions from that accepted route were denounced as "national chauvinism," ensuring a serious conflict and sometimes a gap between the emerging Native Siberian writer and his heritage.

During the first half of the twentieth century, the first generation of Native writers tried to conform to the existing standards but often failed to produce any lasting creative writing. Because of the burden of three revolutions, two wars, and the stark 1930s, early Native Siberian writers, like their North American counterparts of the same period, struggled through catastrophic historical difficulties. Nonetheless, writers such as Nikolai Mordinov (Yakut) and Tyko Vylko (Nenets) managed to produce memorable documentaries, autobiographies, and other expressions of the conflicts and troubles of the times. One must recall also the language problem, which always exists for a Native writer. Written language systems—and thus, literacy—among the Natives of Siberia are an achievement of the Soviet era, but since Russian was the state language, all literature, not to mention education, tended to become Russianized. The Herzen Institute in Leningrad and later the Gorky Writers' Institute in Moscow became centers for Native creative writing programs. This early midcentury period may be considered the beginning of the development of Native Siberian literatures.

The next stage of Native Siberian literatures began in the 1960s, most likely as the Russian response to general global tendencies. Grave matters of ecology, the wholesale advance of industry, and governmental disregard for Native rights on the one hand, and the growing sense of ethnicity on the other, triggered a new wave of ethnic writers who came from all over. The Khirgiz writer Chingiz Aitmatov became the symbol of this new wave. In his famous pieces "The White Steamship" and "The Mangy Dog Running along the Shore" he introduced a sense of tragedy born from frustrated hopes to maintain humanity in the ever-quickening robot-like world of evil and chaos. His words spread worldwide, not only to the Soviet Union. In the North, writers such as Yuri Rytkheu (Chukchee), Vladimir Sangi (Nivkh), and Yuvan Shestalov (Mansi) became leaders of this growing literary movement; in their writing one can trace the turn from the conventional, overoptimistic, predominantly flat, or one-sided view of reality toward the deeper, more alarming, and varying picture of ethnicity, culture, and the world.

Finally, the youngest writers of the subsequent generation were able to bring together new forms and content to articulate not the yesterday of their people but the complexities of today, with the power of intense and individual discourse. Like their colleagues before them, these writers learned their skill in the literary institutes of Moscow and Leningrad, but they lived in a different global reality, culturally and historically. During the notorious *perestroika*, or reform movement, their eyes and mouths were opened. Yeremei Aipin, Yuri Vaella, Galina Keptuke, Gennady Dyachkov, Jansi Kimonko, Anna Nerkagi, Leonty Taragupta, Maria Vagatova, Vladimir Sangi, and Yuri Rytkheu, regardless of career or even age differences, made striking creative contributions that shaped contemporary Native Siberian writing. Because of them ethnic Siberian literatures came of age. Their era began the final stand of traditional cultures against the onslaught of industrialization, since their appearance dramatically coincided with the fall of the Soviet Union and the beginning of the era of wild entrepreneurship and the Russian version of robber barons. Each of these writers exhibits a strong sense of kinship with humanity and all natural phenomena of the Earth at a moment in history poised between creation and destruction. The metaphor of blood and spiritual kinship thus becomes the leading motif in *Morning Twilight* (1990), the epic novel about the Khanty people by Yeremei Aipin:

Demyan lived by hunting birds and beasts, catching fish, and picking berries and cedar nuts for his relatives in the small villages, in the settlement, in town, and elsewhere.... He felt his own life was necessary for others. Without him, the lives of all other people on earth would not be whole. One had to live by his relations, understanding each other. And those who visited him at his hunting grounds always understood this and agreed with his ideas about the mutual law of humanity.

The idea of the present anthology is to bring together, for the first time in English, prominent samples of contemporary Native literatures of Siberia, aiming at a cross-section and a closer acquaintance. The selection is by no means inclusive, but the choices are carefully defined. The compilers looked for authors and pieces vitally necessary in an overview for an English-speaking audience, selections that have already become classics. We also tried to choose works that are aesthetically valid. The goal was to capture the flavor, the scope, and most of all the essence of Native Siberian writing. We wanted to present the variety of important ethnic traditions through the voices of their most important representatives. With the sad exceptions of Kimonko, Dyachkov, and Rytkheu, all of these writers are still living and writing. It is easy to see that each of these writers is deeply connected to a traditional culture; that their discourses reflect a strong sense of the oral tradition; that the pain of their hearts reveals a set of life values now greatly at risk. These values are basic—for them as for us—as they bespeak the preservation and celebration of life, wherever it exists. Reading this kind of literature, we feel the intensity of spirituality of all nations as manifested in the voices of their literary masters.

The stories these Native Siberians tell include the Creation, dim reminiscences of the old days, twentieth-first-century realities, and the Apocalypse, which may be awaiting all of us next door or in our own backyards. In the Native frame of reference, Man is measured by the land, as in Jansi Kimonko's *Where the Sukpai Rushes Along*. Nature encompasses the story of his heart and becomes the point of departure for all life ventures.

Yeremei Aipin articulates the entire gamut of Native ideas, providing a life portrait of the Khanty culture so that we may begin to measure our own life by it. Yuri Vaella aspires to the same goal in his poetry, blending oral and literary traditions. Both authors attempt to reconcile the extremes of human history. In his one-act play included here Gennady Dyachkov concentrates on the essence of moral choices, since the matter of choice is crucial in preserving the links between generations. Galina Keptuke, a descendant of a long line of shamans, voices in "Little America" the death dirge for traditional culture in the modern world. As her title hints, she has Native American parallels in mind, suggesting yet another kind of kinship.

Maria Vagatova's poignant poetic voice seems a piercing cry of sadness and deep love for her Native surroundings and the old ways, yet at the same time a celebration of her people, who will survive despite the millennia of hardships and catastrophes. The writer's career of Yuri Rytkheu, a Chukchee author from the extreme northeastern Chukota Peninsula, includes many books of prose, awards, honorary titles, and distinguished positions, but his real success lies in the evolution of his prose from Soviet propaganda to a synthesis of mytho-legendary and contemporary discourses, especially in his personal psychological dramas, of which the short story "Kakot's Numbers" is the most striking.

Vladimir Sangi, a Nivkh from the Sakhalin Island area of the Pacific shores, is a conflicting product of old and new. Although his political and administrative career was hectic, his writings bespeak a passionate attempt to record the legends and render in print the epics of his people while realistically capturing the life of his Native contemporaries. "My First Shot" is a personal reminiscence of the hardships that the Nivkh community suffered during World War II.

Anna Nerkagi paints a vision of Thanatopsis as the result of all of humanity's misbehavior, whatever the source. The only life-giving force that remains is the power of tradition. The sacred Bear Song, carefully restored and translated from the Khanty by Leonty Taragupta, completes the circle, because the origin of the Bear Feast, the main sacred ceremony of the Khanty, embraces their entire mythology, while suggesting ways to restore world harmony and ensure survival.

Our collection of Native Siberian literature is framed by two invocations of the Evenk people, "To Nature, When the Earth Turns Green" and "To Nature, When the Green Recedes." The Evenks, who number approximately thirty thousand and live in central Siberia, speak the Evenk language, which is composed of three dialects. They are dispersed over extensive areas of the taiga and tundra from the west side of the Yenisei River to the tundra north of the Arctic Circle, between the Yenisei and Lena Rivers, to the southern part of the coast of the Sea of Okhotsk in the east. These seasonal invocations, ancient and anonymous, effectively address various cultures and time periods, across traditional and contemporary experiences.

Academically, Native Siberian writing exhibits by its character a strong relationship to such ethnic creative writers as Chinua Achebe and Wole Soyinka in Nigeria, N. Scott Momaday and the bulk of Native American literatures, Jeannette Armstong and Lee Maracle among the Native writers of Canada, and Rudolfo Anaya and many Chicano authors. These artists bring to our attention the leading cultural issues of our times worldwide. Within ethnic literatures we find the active process of experimenting with narrative discourse, involving and combining traditional (myth, orality, bilingualism) and nontraditional (realistic or beyond) literary techniques.

Every piece collected here is concerned above all with the

idea of kinship. It is ever present, no matter the specific subject. Vaella questions himself—and us—about the dangers of family and clan disintegration, while Aipin elevates the problem to a universal level. Native literatures teach us the power of this wisdom and the consequences that will follow if we abandon the kinship between past and future, fathers and sons, man and his environment, man and his neighbors, individual and community, personality and culture. They provide us with hope that we may hear at last the cry of the wild crane and maintain the way of kinship.

The illustrations for this volume are by two Khanty artists, Nadezda Taligina and Gennady Raishev. Each uniquely demonstrates the visual dimension of his or her Native world as well as the creative discoveries that such a world entails. While Taligina aims to record, ethnographically, the daily life of the Khanty, Raishev strives to render the consciousness of his people: both approaches are crucial now. Taligina and Raishev represent a variety of Native Siberian artists, modern and contemporary, including the traditions of Tyko Vylko, Constantine Pankov, Leonid Lar (all three are Nenets), Semion Nadein (Evenk), among many others.

The goal of *The Way of Kinship* is to move beyond the "first acquaintance" approach to this literature and culture by presenting a comparative teaching manual for courses in ethnic diversity, cultural understanding, cross-cultural studies, and ethnic literatures. Such courses are crucial to the survival of Native traditions in the twenty-first century and indispensable for our own physical and spiritual survival.

Evenk Invocation for Good Fortune

TO NATURE, WHEN THE EARTH TURNS GREEN

(

O Mother Earth, I have come from the expanses of the River Yana, called *Mother*, too, from ancient times. I have come from the valley-dwelling Yakuts, taking refuge on your warm bosom, poor me. I have come here, to where my eyes first saw the world. Dear Mother, I bow down to you and pay my respects, for I tread on your green garment. By this tiny coin, as small as my fingernail, I mark my visit. If only you would lift your eyes from beneath your golden-black brows and look my way, my joy would be boundless.

That is all I have to say. Don't be angry, Mother. My face isn't handsome, my veins are like knots, and my lungs are weak, as you can see for yourself. See how I bow down; see how I crawl on all fours before you, hoping you will mark my visit in some way. I will wait for three days, and no more than seven.

That is all, Mother. I have nothing more to say. Your orphaned children, the deer, are on the move from the very headwaters of the Yana down to its mouth. Out of such wealth, if it pleases you, make us a gift of an animal with hooves. Just one would do!

Yeremei AIPIN (KHANTY)

(

The son of a hunter and fisherman, **Yeremei Aipin** was born in the native village of Varyogan in West Siberia in 1948. Ethnically, he is of the Khanty people, of the Finno-Ugric language stock. As a young man he labored in the Siberian oil fields at the state depository of Samotlor, and as a carpenter before specializing in creative writing at Moscow's State Literary University. Following his graduation in 1976, he spent ten years at the Khanty-Mansiisk Center for the Native Arts. His early writing consisted of translations from Khanty into Russian. His books include *Waiting for the First Snow,* tales (1974); *I Listen to the Earth,* an autobiography (1977); *In the Shadow of an Old Cedar,* tales (1980); *Morning Twilight: A Novel of the Khanty* (1990); *The Oath Breaker,* selected works (1995); *At the Dying Hearth,* nonfiction (1998); and *Mother of God in Bloody Snow,* a novel (2003, filmed in 2009). Aipin has been instrumental in establishing the Native Heritage Park, a museum/memorial sacred-place complex known as Torum Maa (Place of the Gods), in the city of Khanty-Mansiisk.

Much of Aipin's career has been devoted to politics and administration, and he has worked widely on behalf of the Khanty people. From 1993 to 1995 he served as a representative in the state parliament, the Duma. From 1993 to 1997, he was President of the Association of the Indigenous Minorities of the North. He has also served as editor of the monthly newspaper *The Word of the Peoples of the North.* Founded in Moscow in 1993, this news-paper featured a series of his essays, later published in book form as *Destined to Die* in 1994. Currently Aipin is a member of the local Duma at Khanty-Mansiisk. He is also a member of the Writ-ers' Union of Russia. His works have been translated into German, Hungarian, Finnish, and English.

OLD MAN MOON

The copper-red face of the moon floated slowly out of the pines. Everything—the spring snows, the evening clouds, the houses and people—reflected the same purple, copper-red color. When I saw the enormous round face of the moon, I asked my mother:

"Who is that over there?"

My mother answered:

"That is Old Man Moon."

Stunned by its vivid complexion and flaming enormity, I pointed my finger at it, and my mother rebuked me strictly:

"You should never point your finger at the Old Man."

"Why?" I asked.

"Your finger will ache," she explained. "It's a well-known belief." Turning to Old Man Moon, she added: "He doesn't like anyone to point at him. Who would?"

"Must be a strict Old Man," I thought. "I have to be careful with him." I didn't want my longest finger to ache. So I asked my mother what would happen to me now. She said the Old Man would forgive me the first time, because I had acted out of ignorance, not intending any harm. But in the future I mustn't do so. I'd show respect to the celestial Old Man.

So I adhered to this principle as I grew older.

It seemed that Old Man Moon had the likeness of a human being. "He understands me," I reasoned. "Just like people on earth." This strengthened my belief that everything of Heaven and Earth is connected, is one and whole. Which meant that I could live in Heaven as well as on Earth. For the Old Man has lived on Earth, too. Perhaps he's my relative. . . .

(

My godfather Yefrem told me an ancient myth about the origin of the Moon:

Once upon a time there lived a Man. He was happy, but he felt a constant urge to roam. He wanted to see the Earth, what was behind the farthest bog, the farthest house, the farthest hill. He felt sad, and when his wife noticed it, she let him go. So he mounted a horse and departed.

At some point on his journey—we don't know exactly when—he came upon a town. He stopped, left his horse near a house, and went inside, staying with the woman who lived there for some time. But then he felt the same urge again, so he got on his horse and departed. And after a while he came upon another town. He saw a house, and a woman living inside, and stayed with her, too. But time passed and he left yet again; and after wandering for years, his heart ached for home.

So he started homeward. But he'd been away for so long that the town where he'd lived after first leaving his wife no longer existed—it was just a mound of earth, overgrown with a thicket. He dismounted and started to dig at it with his foot, and suddenly his woman jumped out of the mound. "O my dear, my darling!" she cried. "Come here!" And she rushed after him.

The Man jumped on his horse and rode away as fast as he could, but the Underworld woman didn't fall behind; screaming and howling, she followed right after him. Then, when he came to the other town, he saw that it too was no more than a mound, and from it the other woman jumped out. The two of them chased him, and although he was trying his best, they were catching up, almost touching the tail of his horse.

Before long he neared his native land, and in his mind he called with all his might to his original woman: "O my wife, save me!" His wife caught hold of his thought, ran from the house, and caught her husband by the right hand and foot before he had time to get off of his horse. And so a tug-of-war started from opposite sides of the horse—the two women here, his wife there. No one would yield, and finally the Man was torn apart, right down the middle.

The two Underworld women screeched happily, then rushed away with their half and soon vanished.

The Man's wife brought her half into the house and made of it a small child whom she put into a crib and began to nurse, to make him grow. He got larger, grew up, and matured; but he would only stay grown for three days before shrinking into a little baby again. So his wife would nurse him and raise him again, and for three days he would stay grown. Then everything would revert once more. So it went, day and night, until she was too exhausted to move.

Then she said:

"If I had got the half with your heart, I would have made a Man out of you; but as I have the heartless half, I am helpless."

She made a little ball out of her half, went outside, and said: "I couldn't do it, so let the Sky nurse you and harbor you!" With this, she threw the ball high into the sky.

And that ball became the Moon. It grows at first, remains large for three days, and then begins to diminish. And so it goes from month to month, year to year, age to age. And out of respect people began to call the Moon "The Old Man," because he fills the Earth at night with his wonderful light.

And the Man's wife—that first one, his one and only, whom he didn't appreciate enough at the beginning—she didn't want to live on Earth without her beloved, so she went up into the Sky and became the Sun.

(

I had such pity for the Man in godfather Yefrem's story that I wanted to cry. So as not to show it, I kept silent for a long time. Then I demanded:

"Why did she get the half without the heart? Tell me!"

My godfather Yefrem looked at me and explained:

"If she had got the half *with* the heart, there would be no story. Do you see?"

But I didn't want to see. I didn't want a story. I needed the Man *alive,* so he could live close by me, here on Earth. But the elders wouldn't allow that.

I thought a lot about that Man who had been made to suffer. And one day I realized that the women in the myth were Good and Evil. These forces inevitably had to come into conflict, and when they did, they had to tear the Man in half. Still later I understood that inside every man there are two parts— the Light and the Dark. As time passes, one of these prevails. A man will spend the rest of his life under the influence of one of these colors, and all of his acts and thoughts will follow a certain path.

Pondering this, I think more and more often: which of the two will take my heart, the Light or the Dark?

THE EARTH'S PAIN

Whenever by accident my mother touched the earth with an ax, she would quickly level the cut, covering it with woodchips and fir needles. My father would do the same, whenever his ax slipped from a tree and sliced the earth. I once asked my mother the meaning of this.

"It makes a wound on the Earth's body," my mother said. "By no means should you leave Her wounds unattended. It hurts Her!"

"It hurts?" I was astonished. "You never told me that before."

"If by accident you hurt the Earth—our Sitting One—you have to heal the wound instantly. You have to close the cut, so it will heal sooner."

By this time I already knew that I shouldn't repeat too often the sacred name of the one who carries us on Her body—the Earth! On certain occasions, when asking for help, or in times of triumph or danger, this is when to invoke Her by that name, the Earth. But in daily life She is referred to as the Sitting One. Perhaps, I reasoned, the name would wear out, lose color from common use. Therefore children were prohibited to use it vainly. And She herself, if she overheard, was not happy about it.

I remembered my mother's words: everything alive has a soul. Man has a soul. The Bear has a soul, and after feasting and dancing in his honor, we roll up the bearskin and put it back inside the house. The tree, the smallest grass, the flower has a soul. And all who possess it feel pain. So our Earth, perhaps, has a soul, too.

So I asked my mother again:

"Does Her wound hurt Her much?"

"Yes, of course," she answered. "Do you remember when you cut your finger? Did it hurt?"

"Yes!" I cried.

"Well, it's like that with the Sitting One," my mother answered sadly. "Only we don't feel Her pain."

Vividly I imagined the Sitting One. She is a majestic, beautiful lady who sits there while we, the people, live and crawl on Her shoulders; and sometimes, out of ignorance, we hurt Her, bring Her suffering. But She—I imagined Her simultaneously as a person and a deity—forgives us for many of these offenses. For She is as kind and just as my own mother, and She understands when children at play make mischief. It was no wonder they call Her the Sitting Mother. All people on Earth are Her children.

I looked at my mother and thought: she feels the pain of the Sitting Mother, the Earth's pain. Not every human being can sense it, but my mother certainly does. Whenever she accidentally touched the Earth with her ax, I saw the pain on her face.

So I asked:

"Mother, can you feel the Earth's pain?"

She looked at me attentively, was silent for a moment, then said quietly and pensively:

"Sometimes, perhaps."

I didn't understand then about anyone else's pain. Thinking about it later, I perceived that the Root of all living roots goes into the Earth—the root of a tree, the tree itself, its fruit, the smallest bugs and spiders, the birds and beasts, and man himself. Everyone is connected, everything is held by one Root, and this Root goes into the Earth. And whoever wounds the Earth wounds the Root of all roots. And whoever threatens that Root, first and foremost, threatens himself and all of humanity. But that initial pain is only felt by a few, although the final blow is felt by everyone. Every stroke will be felt in the future.

I listened to my mother. And yet another thought came to me. So I asked:

"Mother, when we dig the Earth with a sharp spade, don't we bring Her pain?"

"No, we don't," my mother said with assurance. "When we dig or build out of necessity or with a good purpose, the Earth is happy. For that, She holds nothing against man."

And so I began to think about the reasonable and unreasonable things in this life on Earth.

Meanwhile, my mother explained why it was impossible to hurt our Earth. All kinds of peoples and nations, birds and beasts, and trees and grasses live on Earth. And the Earth holds all of them. Being sacred, She gives life to all. But if you hurt Her and offend Her once and for all—what then? How to live? If there is no Earth, there is no life. Therefore, we must care for the Earth. We must think of Her each day, and mind Her until our last moment.

And this last moment for my mother soon followed, when she went into the Earth.

Since then I have looked with envy upon those who have mothers. Yet it seems they don't regard them with the proper feeling of holiness. Because they don't understand what it means to lose a mother early in childhood. To grow up without a mother. To live without one.

When she was here, it was one world; but without her, it was completely different.

My mother went into the Earth.

And with blackened faces the men, my clansmen, cut the Earth. It was January, and they cut the icy Earth with axes. Cut it in silence. We, my elder sister Lisa and I, sat by the fire and watched them without a tear. All tears had been shed long ago. We sat alone. Other sisters stayed at home, for the youngest of them was only seven months old. She stayed in the cradle, because our custom strictly prohibits bringing children in cradles to the grave.

We sat by the fire while the men cut the Earth. And we

noticed frozen pieces of Earth fall on the blackened snow. They were cutting the Earth my mother loved so much, the Earth she entered so prematurely. And in the morning, after sunrise, she was gone. According to Khanty belief, death after sunrise means an untimely death.

They cut the Earth of my mother. And we felt the pain. And that pain is alive in me still.

PUZZLES OF MY CHILDHOOD
(from *The Long Tail through the Forest*)

O puzzle of mine, puzzle of mine!
Across the forest
a long tail
lies extended, lies quiet.
What is it?

                              (a path in the woods)

O puzzle of mine, puzzle of mine!
A hundred men
by one belt
are all tied up, are all belted.
What is it?

                              (grass tied in a bundle)

O puzzle of mine, puzzle of mine!
The black horse,
the red horse
embrace each other,
caress each other.
What is it?

                              (a kettle on the fire)

O puzzle of mine, puzzle of mine!
Under the water
a hundred eyes
stare vacantly.
What is it?

                              (a fishnet)

O puzzle of mine, puzzle of mine!
Under the water
a lodge neither stands nor lies.
What is it?

(a fish trap)

O puzzle of mine, puzzle of mine!
A furry circle,
a wooly circle
asks for food in the morning,
asks for food in the evening.
What is it?

(a dog with a curved tail)

MORNING TWILIGHT:
A NOVEL OF THE KHANTY

From the INTRODUCTION

... There came the morning to ascend.

And the Man, slowly turning toward the sun with a long glance at the earth, where he had been born and lived to this very day, pulled at the bridle. And the reindeer at the head of the pack took his first step into the sky, and the little pack train began to rise at an angle, unhurriedly, as if climbing a mountain. Behind its master, the dog guided the flock of reindeer, and it too ascended, following an invisible track in the morning sunlight.

The Man rose into the sky with his wife and two sons.

And for seven days the Earth-dwellers watched as they made their way higher into the sky—watched them unharnessing the reindeer at evening, putting up the tipi or *choom,* watched the dim smoke rising from the smoke-hole, the *makodan.* They watched them come out in the morning, the dog driving the herd of reindeer around its master so he could throw the lariat on the leader's horns. Watched them get under way, then stop to rest after one deer's run, then stop for the night again, to go forth in the morning into an unknown expanse of heaven.

Every day the Earth-dwellers saw them diminish, going farther and farther, higher and higher. And on the seventh day they were gone. Maybe they had reached their destination, or simply exceeded the limits of human sight.

Thus the Ascension of Man was brought to pass.

And the ancient elders relate that several years after the Ascension the Earth-dwellers came together for a feast on the

Sacred Hill. And at the very beginning of the feast the two grown-up sons of the Risen Man appeared. They stopped above the treetops, and the tribesmen called to them:

"Come down to see us!"

"We can't come down to Earth!" the brothers answered. "If we do, there'll be no way for us to return!"

They explained that below the treetops, on the Earth itself and just above the Earth, there was too much *uncleanliness*. It could be seen much better from above. The Earth, they said, is wrapped in a misty, dusty, unclean cloud, which those who dwell below don't even suspect. And if the Risen Man would enter that cloud, he would be destined to remain on Earth forever.

The Earth-dwellers understood this—maybe even suspected it—and stopped trying to persuade the two heavenly visitors. But the brothers willingly talked to the tribesmen, telling them about their life in heaven. And they observed all of the rituals on the Sacred Hill—bowing to all the gods and goddesses of the Earth and Sky who had been invited to the great feast. They said their father and mother were well; that they sent their regards to their native land; that their household was in order; that they were living according to the ways of the Upper World.

After the feast was over, the sons of the Risen Man bade farewell to their tribesmen, got on their sledges, and flew back to their world above the clouds.

Henceforth there was no news from them, nor did they reappear. But their memory remained—in the form of a single larch sledge of the Risen Man, overgrown with moss and grass, which on the day of his departure had sunk deep into the ground.

Earlier, the Man had told his wife to give all the things they wouldn't need to the tribesmen and relatives who would remain on Earth. She should take with her nothing extra or unclean. But she didn't obey. She left nothing for the people but packed all of their possessions into the last sledge in the train. At the moment of departure, she touched her pack's head reindeer with her guiding rod. And the pack carried her up, following the clear track of her husband, a track unnoticed to the casual eye in the frosty early-morning air. The reindeer lifted the first sledge of her train, then the second, then the third, gliding as if on new snow through the sky's transparent plain.

But then the sledges stopped short, and the woman looked back. The last sledge, carried by the two strongest bucks, couldn't get off the ground. All of the bridles, down to the first sledge, were taut, the entire train straining with the effort. With a final push, the sledge finally left the snowy ground, the bucks tightening their powerful backs, desperately trying to leap, slowly and heavily raising the sledge into the sky. One more jump! Yet another, then the harness straps snapped, and the sledge plummeted, landing in the very middle of the frozen forest.

The Sky refused to accept a sledge full of unclean possessions.

So the people went into the Sky without their last sledge.

Since that day, many winds and rains have passed on earth. And people say that the remains of that sledge can still be seen. The sledge was made from the strongest and most durable tree in the taiga forest—the larch tree—rendering time itself powerless to destroy it, to turn it to dust. The larch sledge was left to posterity as a lesson: so the people would not take with them anything superficial or unclean, so all deeds and thoughts upon their road—called the life way—would be selfless and clean. So future generations would make a clean track. . . .

Isn't that the essence of life? Isn't that the truth of the Earth and the human race? And to grasp this truth, must we really see the larch sledge of the Risen Man? Must we really journey, land after land, to an unknown country? If they have not built a city nearby, or a railroad, or an oil-drilling station, I'm sure this larch tree sledge is still there, its high brow half sunk into the Earth as a monument to the Ascension of Man, and a memento of my risen tribesman. . . .

From CHAPTER 3

Demyan lived by hunting birds and beasts, catching fish, and picking berries and cedar nuts for his relatives in the small villages, in the settlement, in town, and elsewhere. Everything he planned he did unhurriedly, with an eye to the future. He felt his own life was necessary for others. Without him, the lives of all other people on earth would not be whole. One had to live by his relations, understanding each other. And those who visited him at his hunting grounds always understood this and agreed with his ideas about the mutual law of humanity. Only Anisya, his wife, didn't take his words seriously and would spite him.

"What do you get from your relatives?" she would ask.

"What do I need?" Demyan would answer. "I don't need much, except for understanding!"

"You don't need much, because nobody gives you anything for free! What if we didn't have enough deer for the sledge? We need reindeer!"

"I wouldn't take the deer. Everybody needs them. You yourself know that there are hunters who have even fewer deer than we do. And what else? I have no use for a car."

"What an idea!" Anisya laughed. "Nobody'd offer you a car. Given a car, you'd want a plane or a helicopter next time!"

A sudden thought seized Demyan.

"But we have a plane!" He smiled at his wife. "The city provides the plane! It flies from the city to the village, carrying people! We have a plane!"

"But it's not free. It takes money to fly!" Anisya stopped him short.

That's a woman for you, Demyan thought. She'd out-talk anybody.

"You're the only one who gives anything to your relatives!" Anisya said. "But people are different. Few are like that! Few!"

"Let me tell you about the plane," he reasoned with his

wife. "They don't take pelts from me for nothing. They give me money. Now, if I would give my pelts for free, a plane would fly me for free! Right? And the same pelts would be in the store!"

"Have you become a communist already, doing without money?" she poked again. "Ahead of everyone, all by yourself?"

"What if I *were* a communist? How am I to blame?"

"Well, it must be hard all by yourself," she mocked.

"It must be hard for *you,* since you refuse to understand." Demyan was stubborn. "Yet people understand. One should live by his relations."

Anisya fell silent. Demyan didn't consider it quarreling when they talked like that. When his wife didn't agree, she simply kept silent. He felt her resistance and pitied her a little. But he couldn't give in to her, partly because the war had taken his father and all three of his brothers. He couldn't afford to think in terms of personal profit, that they had died for the sake of two immediate relatives—for him and his mother.

Their four lives for these two. It was too much, yet too little. It couldn't be. It wasn't so. But deep inside Demyan understood that they had fallen in battle for him and his mother, for all of the relatives in the villages and cities, for all of humanity. And the best memory of them was the people who remained, for whom they had died, people who were closer to him now.

His three brothers and his father-soldier—they were in their graves now in far-off neighboring lands, not in the tribal cemetery at Little Yar, with all of their ancestors to the tenth generation. The head of the local administration had been the last one to see them alive. And Demyan looked to this man, this veteran, as if he harbored a tiny particle of their breath, their lust for life, their love of kin and native land. And when this veteran himself died, Demyan felt again the same frightening emptiness. A connection with the world, with humanity, had been lost, as if his father and brothers had died a second time.

He felt abandoned in this emptiness, helpless and unneeded. And when his mother died soon after the war, he experienced the same feeling yet again, as he had in childhood when the war took his father and brothers. For they had been his connection to the world, to the past and future, and this connection had been abruptly cut—the first shock of his life.

After the veteran died, Demyan looked desperately for a way out of his emptiness. One had to live somehow, to restore somehow the severed relationships with the world, with life itself. And the relationship was restored by Anisya, the veteran's younger daughter. Earlier, he hadn't seen much of her. She was at school, then went away somewhere for a long while. When he met her again, he had a dim feeling that great changes were in store. And although she had more fortunate suitors, she chose him, who at that time looked awkward and gloomy.

Why him? He couldn't say to this day. Because back then he had wandered blindly everywhere, without care or a place to stay. And he had lacked that spiritual balance, that feeling of oneness with the world—the unity of human mind and living nature, the unity of all being that would come to him later. He couldn't tell for sure then what feelings he had for Anisya. There was only a great attachment and respect for her father. But when he got to know her better, he was happy she had chosen him, not somebody else.

Then the children came, and the feeling of emptiness went away.

This is how the lost relationship with the past and future, with the Earth and Sky, was restored.

Years later, by insisting that Demyan should think first only of himself, Anisya helped him make a discovery. His relatives lived in every village and town, over the entire planet, his connection with humanity and the Universe. He felt assured that this connection would never be broken. It was an everlasting relationship no one could ever shatter.

A man has many blood relatives in his past and future, Demyan reasoned. Every living person has four grandparents. Which means eight great-grandparents and sixteen great-great-grandparents. And if you take this great-great ten times, you get more than four thousand relatives. The deeper you go into the past, the more relatives you have. And, of course, the roots of every small nation—say, of only several hundred people—go deep into other nations. And doesn't this mean all nations are relatives to each other? And is this bad? Certainly no one would say so.

Demyan taught this idea, about the relationship of all peoples on earth, to his children as they grew up. And once, his elder son, Mikul, said:

"Yes, I know the Khanty have relatives in other countries and lands."

"Who told you?"

"A teacher at school who spoke to us about languages."

"And what did she say about our relatives?"

"She said that the closest nations to Khanty are the Mansi and Hungarians. They are related by language."

"Mansi live close by," his father said. "And the Hungarians live somewhere far away."

"Yes, on the Danube River. That's far." And his son began to tell the story:

"A long time ago we lived together as one people. This was really long ago—in the most ancient of ancient times, as the Khanty say. Then war came. Perhaps several wars, and the people split into two groups. One went to the Danube, the other came here, up North."

His son was silent for a while, then added:

"Scholars think—I've read about it in books—that previously we rode on horses, had cows and sheep, and lived in towns."

"I know," his father said.

"Where from?" Mikul was amazed. "How could you know?"

"Well, take our longer tales and songs. The people in them live in big cities, ride horses, tend cows, make war. There are knights and kings, and there is the *urtaet,* the war leader. In almost every story there is the sea, and the people in the tales sail beyond it."

"True!" his son agreed. "I never paid attention to that before."

"To this day, according to our elders, the greatest sacrifice to God is *lav,* the horse." Demyan remembered the ancient custom. "Next comes *mas,* the cow, the most honored of all domestic animals. The *lav* and the *mas.* The reindeer comes last. All of this must have come to us from afar. From the times when we had towns, horses, cows, and lived in other lands . . ."

"In those times we were called the *Ugri,*" his son added. "And we must have had a common language with the Hungarians, because to this day we share many words."

"Such as?"

"*Sam, kesh, ver, hool . . .*"

And Demyan repeated after his son: "Eye, knife, blood, fish . . ."

"There are also words that are very similar in both languages. We say *lav* for horse, and they say *lo*; dry is *sarm*; for them it is *saraz.* For us, crane is *torh*; for them, *daru.* The house—*hot* and *haz*; the arm—*kaet* and *kez.*"

"You speak as if you knew the language of our relatives from the Danube River!" Demyan was astonished. "Where did you learn it? From books?"

"I learned the words from a scholar, Eva Schmidt. She's a postgraduate student in Budapest. She came to our village and gave a talk at our school. She told us about her own country, about our relationship with them."

"She spoke in our language?"

"Yes, she speaks it."

"Where did she learn it?" Demyan was amazed.

"What do you mean, where? She learned it at home!"

"But how?"

"Through books, of course. She's a philologist."

"A phi-lol-o-gist?" Demyan repeated.

"A person who studies languages and literature."

"Eva. *Eve*," Demyan said. "Well, the name of this woman scholar is very similar to our Khanty name *Evi*, or girl. What else did she say? What else was she interested in?"

"She's recorded tales and songs, legends and traditions. Everything interests her. The way we live, what we sing . . ."

"How many relatives a man has!" Demyan said. "Amazing!"

"And she told us about other relatives of ours," Mikul continued. "Those who live in the Baltic countries, on the seashore. They include the Estonians, the Finns, the Saami, the Korela, the Veps . . ."

"On the seashore, you say? I've heard of them," Demyan said. "The elders used to say that, in the most ancient of ancient times, during the calamity of the Great Waters, many people who tried to escape on rafts were scattered throughout the world. When the waters receded, the people stayed in the countries where the water had carried them. The elders call them the People Carried Away by the Great Waters. Before that, everyone lived together. This is what our tradition says."

Demyan was silent, then said to his son:

"Your ways and roads will carry you farther than mine. You shall see many of our relatives." He stressed the last word. "Be a good relative yourself."

And his son understood. He would remember his father's words many years later when he befriended Ferentz Keresti, a Hungarian engineer, who had come to construct electronic equipment for processing field materials for oil and gas exploration. Keresti—whose equipment helped dispel the mystery of the depths of the Khanty and Mansi land—took an interest in the life and spirituality of the native people he met. When he returned home, he relayed his impressions to his own people. Then Mikul received a magazine from Budapest, *New Mirror,* with Ferentz's essay "Our Siberian Relatives."

But that would come later. Right now, Demyan was contemplating his connection to humanity. He needed this connection badly, more than life itself. Even more so, since he had died with his brothers near Moscow in 1942. And was blown up again by a stray artillery shell, with his younger brother, at the bank of Lake Balaton in 1945. And the bullet that entered his father's body in Berlin, in April 1945, pierced his own heart, too. He had been killed four times, with his father and brothers, and many times more with other relatives. Therefore, in order to survive and not vanish in a void, he needed a close kinship with humanity. Without such a kinship he could not live on this earth.

But now, listening to the sound of his sledge as he headed out to the forest, he felt something threatening this kinship with the world. It wasn't clear what it was; everything seemed dim, as in a mist. And his restlessness grew, but he could do nothing about it. He couldn't shut it down with a command, as he could his howling dog, Harko.

A long life in the taiga forest had sharpened Demyan's senses. His perception was keen; he could foresee changes in nature, and through them the events of human life. His feelings never failed him. And he would have been happy, this time, to admit he was wrong, but he knew he was right: he had a bad feeling about the newest relatives—the explorers, the *seekers,* as he called them. Well, no relatives were ideal. People were different everywhere. But the seekers, he had heard, were to blame for certain things. Yet who is without sin? Not many. Only the gods of Heaven and Earth, perhaps. But the myths say that the gods themselves were crafty, that they played tricks and pranks, and acted like children. . . .

Passing the marsh, Demyan entered the main road, called the Czar's Road from time immemorial. It stretched along the bank of the Mother River, through pine forests from East to West, connecting two villages, the Lower and Upper. By this road people went into the City on the right bank of the Ob River, to deliver their furs and fish. Other roads branched from it toward smaller hunting households.

The head deer, Vondyr, turned eastward by himself, as if knowing where his master was going. And Demyan went on, his thoughts flying like birds, now forward, now backward, into the depths of time, then into the present again. Soon, accompanied by the melody of the sledge, which seemed squeaky and sharp, he came to Spring Lake. And here, from deep inside, first sprang the black fire that began to lick at his heart.

He saw clearly that a great swath had been cut through the surrounding forest, like an arrow, and the tip of this arrow pointed to his winter grounds nearby—several smaller marshy lakes, and a pinewood. Here were both house and pasture. And he remembered what the hunters from the Lower village had said, for the seekers had arrived there already:

First, they let the cutters come with their axes and saws, and they cleared out a broad, straight line. Machines with steel drills followed, biting into the taiga. People in the know spoke of wondrous devices that captured the breath of the Earth and helped listen to its depths, impenetrable to the hunter's eye or ear.

They followed a sheet of paper, which they called a map, featuring the face of the Sacred Earth—the lakes and rivers, forests and marshes, groves and springs, the taiga hills and hollows. This map depicted Demyan's winter house and its corral, and the pointed-roof plank shed—the fish house—where fish and meat and hunting gear were stored. The paper marked as well the family Woodland River, the Yuhan-Yagun, which empties into the long gulf that penetrates the mainland. On the higher, right bank of Yuhan-Yagun lies the Spring Village of the clan, the little timber houses covered with birch bark. Behind them stand the *labazes* on wooden pillars, the storehouses for winter clothing and food. A little in front of them sit the sheds and smokehouses, all under birch bark roofs, and in front of the doors, the clay ovens for baking bread. At the landing are the overturned boats and *oblas*, the canoes, and the poles for nets.

The same map must have noted the Summer Village, too, on the left bank of the river, where on the sandy beach near the woods stood thin plank houses, the summer *labazes* and ovens, the same sheds and smokehouses.

If so, the Fall Village had been marked, too, on the big stream at the Marsh Side, under the century-old pines on the steep sandy rise. An entire town stood there, with well-built houses and all necessary storage buildings. Demyan used to see such maps, featuring the face of Mother Earth. They took in everything. And as he had come to believe on many occasions, those who made them didn't make mistakes. These seekers, too, must have been very precise—and now they were aiming straight at *him*.

In a week or two they would come to his winter grounds; they would cut down the pine forests, the cedar woods, the birch groves near the Woodland River, and if a village got in the way, they would cut it down, too. As the hunters said, the seekers don't deviate from their route, to the left or right. Where it is marked for them to drill, they drill, fifteen or twenty meters deep. Then they put something inside, which explodes like gunpowder deep into the earth, the Sitting One. And this is only the beginning. After these seekers, new ones come, more powerful than the first. They drill the earth kilometers deep. And if they find oil, *the fat that burns,* still others come—the extractors.

Demyan had been told that the extractors were the worst. They literally turned the forest upside down, from the white mosses and black *urmans*—the ancestral homes of the local gods—to the endless marshes. People said these seekers and extractors boasted of leaving nothing alive for ten kilometers on either side of their way. Demyan didn't want to believe it. But they had so many machines! What if you turned them all against the taiga, against bird and beast—wouldn't the very Earth groan? What ground would have the power to withstand them, to overcome them? In winter, for instance, when the snow is deep, you can take moose with your bare hands. And with sky machines and earth machines—no trouble at all! Not for ten kilometers around, or for hundreds. You could finish off everything. And they say that's exactly what happened a long time ago to the hunters downriver.

Yet Demyan had lived quietly thus far, his grounds in the far off wilderness. True, the river delta was touched by the pipeline in the east, by oil in the south, the railroad in the west. The circle was closing in on him, but he himself had not yet been disturbed. Yet the circle was closing in. Only in the north, between the pipeline and the new road, was all quiet. But there the Nenets tundra began, and the divide was nearby. The rivers were already beginning to flow northward, to empty into the Polar Sea. He could feel the sea's breath sometimes in the fall or spring.

Demyan continued on in his sledge, thinking again and again about the past and the future. And the black fire gradually spread through his insides. No cold—no snow or ice on the Earth that had nurtured him and his kin—could quench it. The Earth had to nurture his descendants, too. Yet the sharp pain inside wouldn't release him, even for a minute. All other concerns were set aside, everything was pushed aside by the great swath through the forest that was pointing at his heart.

And he had many concerns. Consider the deer—how many troubles they had brought him! Only three years ago there had been three herds in his pasture. Like any hunter, each fall Demyan would remove three or four teams for hunting. In the spring, after the season was over, he would return these reindeer to the herd. But then the herd was no more. Part of it had gone for meat, another part was sold to hunters, and the rest were driven to the neighboring river, to another division of their co-op game-producing farm. And in a year, these too were gone. Some gossips said that the local director had been pushing for a medal, so he decided to overstock all the oil towns and settlements with deer meat. But he had calculated poorly and soon was displaced, either for this or some other mean deed.

Well, they had got rid of him, but they couldn't get the reindeer back.

And now they were blaming the oil people for laying out their roads on top of the best land—the priceless white moss forests and black *urmans*. With their machines they upturned the *yagel*-mosses, which served as deer food, or they burned them with fires. And without any trace of conscience they chased the deer down with dogs, or shot them with guns, or finished them off by terrorizing them with helicopters.

Yet Demyan considered all this in slightly different terms. His own people were to blame, too—the heads of administration, the deer herders, the hunters. When the master is bad, he thought, he finds someone else to blame.

Yes, there were machines, dogs, guns, and 'copters. He didn't approve of these oil people. But those who fly 'copters, who point the dogs, who raise the guns—they are reasonable people who possess speech; they are not machines. Everything could be discussed with them agreeably, as among relatives. Wouldn't they understand that in the North everything depends on the deer? The Earth needs the deer, the hunter does, the fisherman, even the oilman. They could understand; they would. All they needed was good instruction—all of those newcomers—to teach their bosses, their wives, their children. Even their dogs. Because the main prey, Demyan knew, was not the deer, nor the birds and beasts, but the oil, the fat that burns, in the Earth, which is of no use to reindeer. So let the oil people drill, only without doing harm.

The Earth is large, Demyan knew. If approached as a relative, it would provide for everybody—hunter, deer, oilman. From time immemorial the Khanty had maintained that the Earth is sacred, that it belongs to all living people together, and to no one in particular. The worst evil was to quarrel over the Sitting One. One must not quarrel over Her, but worship Her, the Sitting Mother. She Herself knows how many people, birds and beasts, fishes and insects to carry on Her shoulders. She can estimate Her power well.

Yes, the Sacred Earth should be enough for everybody! The problem was, things weren't going as they should among the relatives. The deer were the first to disappear. If it continued, the birds and beasts would be pushed out, and the fishes from their watery kingdom. And then the time would come for man himself.

Even now it was hard for the hunter to go about without deer. It was expensive to buy one. Last fall, Demyan had heard, the price of a doe had risen to one hundred and fifty rubles. New snows brought new prices. The hunter's budget for the winter was six hundred rubles, the annual income for an average person, enough to buy one team. But what about your family? Where to get clothing? The reindeer served as transportation, food, and clothing. For centuries he had carried, fed, and clothed the Bear tribesmen, the Beaver and Moose kinsmen, as well as others. And now?

What a time we live in, Demyan thought. The only thing to do is to get into the harness yourself!

From CHAPTER 19

"Where is the gold?" Bloody Eye asked in a whistling half-whisper. "Where's your gold? Where's the money? You must tell me!"

Nerm-iki—old man Stepan Sardakov—had kept silent for three days in a row. Bending his head to one side, his tired eyes half-closed, he stood motionless before Bloody Eye, as if he did not see or hear him. He, the father of the postman Kurpelak Galaktion, was no shaman, no prince; neither Elder nor *kulak*—one of the village bourgeoisie. He had not fought for the White Guard during the Civil War, hadn't served as a guide, hadn't helped with the deer teams, and had never committed any crime against the Soviet Power in word or deed. Everyone certainly knew that. As well as Bloody Eye.

But at the beginning of the century, his branch, or *sir*, of Sardakov's clan, had been considered the richest on the River—more than four hundred deer pastured at the headwaters of the Yaguriah. They went out to trade in the Ob cities of Surgut, Berezov, Obdorsk. And the wife that he arranged for his only son—a handsome, big-breasted young woman—was also from the Ob Khanty. That's why they later called her *Asnae,* the Woman from Ob.

After the Civil War the herd had declined in numbers. Some died from disease, some were taken by the collective farm. The remaining deer were finished off during World War II—the Great Patriotic War. The family was big, with many mouths to feed. The grandchildren were growing up, the daughters needed help. They had to survive. And they did. Then the war ended and the times called for strict measures. At the peak of the hunting season hunters were prohibited to leave their hunting grounds, so as not to lose priceless hunting days.

Nerm-iki, because of his age, was a coachman, or *kayur,* at the farm. He brought produce from the headwaters of Amputa, where the people of the Khanty *sir* of Kazamkin were hunting with the bordering Nenets *sirs* of Iusi and Aivaseda. These were the farthest hunting grounds, several days distant from the settlement. The hunters had exhausted their supplies yet couldn't leave without permission. Supplies were to be brought to them by Nerm-iki, and he was in a hurry to do so, in a great hurry. But he was kept in the settlement by Bloody Eye, and his hopes for the road were done for. Bloody Eye wanted gold. He said that Nerm-iki's ancestors had accumulated much gold, which he had inherited. Therefore he, Stepan Sardakov, must have hidden the gold, so as not to give it to the Soviet Power. On the very first day the old man had patiently tried to explain that, yes, his *sir* had been rich at one time, had had many deer and brought them to market in the Ob cities. But this was the only wealth, the deer, and they were long gone. There was no gold whatsoever. Nobody was interested in gold. Who needed gold in the taiga forest? What people had no use for they didn't acquire. What was the use of keeping something for which you had no need? Decoration? Well, perhaps the women had had some trinkets before, but these too were gone, lost during the hard times. It was no joke surviving three wars.

Gifts for the Gods? The gold? You'd have to ask them yourself. A man cannot speak for the Gods.

But Bloody Eye stuck with it—*gold!* He didn't want to hear of anything else. So the old man's face darkened and he went silent, as if frozen. He knew only too well the grip of Bloody Eye. It was a death grip. For good reason they called him the Lowly Spirit, the Black Head of the Underworld, where he brought the people whose souls he had taken.

"Where is the gold?!" he shouted again, his bloody eye gleaming.

He had many faces, like a supernatural being. He could be an Unclean Spirit, setting snares with his sweet little voice for an unsuspecting victim. He could burn every living thing with black lightning. Or he could go berserk, grabbing his little rifle—his revolver or pistol—cracking heads with the butt, shooting through the ceiling, through the icy windows of the hut, through people themselves. He was called the One with the Little Rifle, and there was no quarter from it—everything was done in a flash.

"The gold!" the One with the Little Rifle roared and put his revolver on the table.

Nerm-iki stared blankly in front of him. His wind-beaten face remained motionless.

"You don't give it to me—I'll finish off the whole of your kin!" He banged the butt of the gun on the table. "By the roots! By the roots!"

The old man was silent.

"A-ah-h, the old Khanty dummy!" The revolver's muzzle pointed into the old man's chest. "Bring the gold! Or I'll shoot you like a dog!"

The old man didn't even stir. And then Bloody Eye, turning back into the Lowly Spirit, hissed in a half-whisper:

"I'll begin with your daughters . . ."

He grinned triumphantly and fixed his bloody eye on the motionless face of the old man, who, it seemed, had not yet grasped the sense of his words. Merrily, he added:

"Yes, with your daughters. What is dearer to you—your gold or your daughters? I'll do it, I will! It'll be nicer than talking to you, killing time addressing an old stump! Haw, haw, haw! I think I'll begin with the younger. That beauty, Fedosya . . ."

Nerm-iki winced and raised his head. His anguished eyes met the wall. In front of him, to the left and right, were the walls. The window was behind. And through that window the heavy rectangle of night seemed to squeeze the back of his head.

His children would be interrogated. But what could they tell about gold they'd never seen or heard of?

"Then I'll have to start with your elder one—he, he, he!" The One with the Little Rifle walked around the old man, putting his arms behind him with self-satisfaction. "Just look at her—she can haul wood on her back! Oh ho! Then I'll get to your one-legged puppy, your son. I'll fix him—he'll start dancing! He'll be grateful for the rest of his days, no better doctor for him!"

The old man caught the bloody eye of the Lowly Spirit and said, with heavy weight on each word:

"They . . . don't know . . . anything . . ."

"Where is the gold? The gold!"

The old man raised his hand slowly, touched his white hair with his gnarled fingers, and sighed:

"Here is my gold."

"Get the gold. Or I'll take your kin!"

"Take my head instead."

"I'll have your head anyway!" The One with the Little Rifle laughed. "No need to rush. You give me the gold—I'll set you free. With your head on your shoulders."

They stared at each other face to face. It was quiet. Finally, the One with the Little Rifle turned to the window, wearily waved his hand, and murmured:

"Okay. You may go. We'll continue tomorrow."

The old man turned away slowly and, just as slowly, went out.

At the tiny corner of the farm's meetinghouse, his family awaited him. He didn't touch his meal, just drank a mug of tea. All of them understood that the entire family was in trouble. They exchanged a few words, then fell silent.

It was dark.

"I'll go to him," said the youngest one, Fedosya.

"No!" The old man cut her off firmly. "You have your life ahead of you."

"O, kind *Torum*, where are you?" groaned the elder one, Anisya. "Don't you see our grief? Where are you?"

The one-legged son, Kurpelak Galaktion, sighed heavily.

Then the children of old man Stepan were summoned into

the settlement in connection with "their father's case." They were not allowed to go anywhere without permission from the One with the Little Rifle. Among themselves they called him That One. The women especially were afraid to call him by name.

"He's more powerful than *Torum*," Galaktion said. Then he turned to his older sister. "Now, stop that, Anisya."

Anisya suppressed a heavy groan.

There were no plank beds, no bunks. They had to sleep on the floor, putting down rags.

When they had settled in, Old Man Stepan said quietly:

"His mind hates the ancient roots of our *sir*, he wants to tear them out. But he won't touch you. Sleep well."

He did not sleep himself. Listening to the uneven breathing of his grown-up children and carefully checking their covers, he spent the night by his crippled son and his youngest child, Fedosya. The elder daughter had recently been married to a good fellow of the Kazamkin clan—her life was taking shape. She was good at everything, fast and able, and strong in character. But his son, being a cripple, faced a difficult time. He couldn't spend his entire life under his father's wing. One must make one's own way. And what about Fedosya? What of her fate? She alone wasn't settled in this life. O kind *Torum*, give her a decent bridegroom, a good man! Like her sister, don't let her be alone for too long. Do send her a fine man, O kind *Torum*.

The gloomy dusk came. They lit a dim fire. The tiny corner of the collective farmhouse sprang to life.

"I'll go check the deer," Old Man Stepan said. "We didn't yesterday."

At the door he looked back at his children and smiled guiltily, then added in a cheerful tone:

"I'll be back soon."

And out he went.

His cheerfulness comforted his children. He must be getting over it, they thought. Perhaps all would turn out well.

Soon the sun came up, but the Old Man didn't return. The

One with the Little Rifle was the first to get worried. He sent the younger one, Fedosya, to find out why her father was late from the pasture.

Fedosya, seized with foreboding, half ran to the familiar pasture, slowing down only at a rise leading to the little forest grove, where she stopped short, seeing her father's sledge. Nearby, wrapped in a deer hide with his feet protruding, lay her father. Had he fallen asleep? Was he still asleep? In tears and unable to move, Fedosya began to call her father in a half-whisper:

"*Achi!...Achi!...* Father!... Father!... Hey, *Achi!*"

He didn't respond. Fedosya came nearer, saw the butt of the gun showing from under the hide, and fainted.

For a long time afterward, Fedosya was ill, but she later recovered and returned to the world of the living, marrying Demyan's cousin, Michael the Small. She lived well. But like her elder sister, she was barren, denied the happiness of motherhood until the end of her days.

And Bloody Eye only banged his fist on the table. To think of it! He had been fooled by this old Khanty! Nothing to be done!

That is how the father of Galaktion the One-Legged, the ancient root of the Sardakov's *sir,* departed this life....

〈

When he traveled, Bloody Eye loved entertainment. His favorite "game" was what he called Cutting the Hair of the Shaman, or the Shooting Range. Once, when he went to a local governmental town with old man Yefrem, blood brother to Demyan's father, he ordered the outfit to stop at the edge of the family forest, on Sandy Lake before the river Neh, and told old man Yefrem to stand in the middle of the frozen lake. Then he drew his gun, blew a hair from the muzzle, checked the barrel in a business-like way, stepped back several feet, and, half-turning as in a duel, slowly began to raise his arm.

All was quiet.

Even the deer caught their breath.

The coachmen froze at their sledges.

Then a shot resounded.

Old Man Yefrem stood exactly as before, a bit of fur from the hood of his parka, cut by the bullet, floating to his feet in the frosty air.

The echo rolled over the snows of the lake and was lost without a trace somewhere in the pines.

The echo gone, the quiet returned.

Another shot resounded.

More fur floated from the old man's hood.

And the new echo died.

In this way Bloody Eye trimmed the hood of Old Man Yefrem. With a single round he trimmed the edges, while fur floated all around. When the gun was empty, he took out another round and, loading it, went up to the old man and said with a grin:

"Well, give thanks to my arm and eye!"

The old man stood motionless.

"Are you paralyzed, or what? Gone speechless?"

The old man was silent still.

"Have you bitten off your tongue? Don't want to talk to me, eh?"

Silence.

"Serves you right! This is different from playing games with your gods! Do you understand who has the power?"

The face of the old man was motionless.

"Why don't you beg for mercy? Why don't you cry? Why don't you fall on your knees? *Why?* Don't you feel any fear?"

"Your mind's no bigger than your little finger," Old Man Yefrem said quietly.

Bloody Eye stirred. "How so?"

"My breath is in the hands of *Numi Torum,* supreme god of

the Khanty." The old man nodded at the sky. "I am in my six-
ties now. I have lived. And if I am destined to die on this very
spot, by your hand, I shall not take one step away. I shall die
here. And nothing or nobody will help me. Nothing can save
me. Even you . . . But if I still have more days to live, you shall
not take my breath away. You'll do nothing to me, whether you
want to or not. I'll live. Your mind's no bigger than your little
finger."

"What's my mind got to do with it?"

"That's not for you to understand," the old man said.

Grave silence.

Old Man Yefrem didn't know then that he would return in
two years; that he would become the elder on the River; that
he would live a hundred years; that he would be one of a few to
outlive his tormentor.

Suddenly Bloody Eye grinned, showing his yellow fangs.
Putting his gun back into his holster, he said, either in amazement or admiration:

"Powerful, aren't you, you devil!" And he went back to the
sledges.

And it wasn't clear whom he meant—*Numi Torum* or Old
Man Yefrem.

〉

The following story was told to Demyan by an old Nenets man,
Yapta Vaella:

Bloody Eye had been interrogating Sam-iki—Old Man
Eye—from the Moose clan. "I was called to act as a translator,"
Yapta Vaella recalled. "I knew Khanty very well. There were
three of us in the room—Bloody Eye, Sam-iki, and me.

"After some time Bloody Eye stopped in front of Sam-iki
and said this:

" 'Many, many shamans have I seen! From all of the rivers!
Had business with them all. But not a single one could cope

with me. I am the most powerful of all. . . . They say you are the greatest shaman on this river. If so, show me your shaman's power. Show me something, so I will believe.'

"I translated his words.

"Sam-iki was silent.

"'Well, I am Bloody Eye, and you are just an Eye,' That One said. 'We are almost relatives. Can I be more powerful? Come on! Don't be afraid, nothing bad will happen. Demonstrate your shamanic craft. Or can it be that you're powerless?'

"Sam-iki remained silent.

"'So, this means you cannot? A weakling, eh? A pity, that!' I translated this, too, and the Lowly Spirit was grinning.

"Then Sam-iki quietly raised his arms to the level of his chest, pressed his elbows tight, and began to roll on his feet, began to dance on the spot. And we noticed that, on his right, his knife had come out of its sheath.

"It came out by itself.

"And the knife floated in the air, its blade facing front. The knife went toward Bloody Eye, and his face became as white as a birch tree, then totally bloodless, as white as snow. I saw it clearly, for he was standing right in front of me.

"The knife went slowly around him.

"I saw that with my own eyes, these very eyes.

"The knife circled around him and went back into the sheath. By itself.

"The knife came back to its master, from the other side. They were inside an invisible circle drawn by the knife. The two stood frozen.

"I stared with wide eyes at the knife's handle, and at Sam-iki. His hands were up as before. He hadn't touched the knife. Never have I seen anything like this in my life.

"For a long while Bloody Eye stood speechless.

"Sam-iki was silent, too.

"And I was silent. Everything was silent.

"Then Bloody Eye ran into the street. Without his coat. Into the cold. And when he opened the door, the smoky white cold came in.

"I didn't know what to do.

"Soon he returned, though. With a bottle of vodka and half a loaf of bread. Well, he had gone to the store, I understood. The store was quite near, just opposite the farm's guesthouse, where the bakery is now.

"First he poured for Sam-iki. And Sam-iki drank. Then he poured for himself and drank it up, too. Then he tore off a piece of bread and gave it to Sam-iki. And Sam-iki took the bread.

"I didn't know what to do. I knew I'd better get out of there. But I couldn't go without permission from That One. Because you never knew what path his mind would take, where it would turn, what it would do next.

"He had forgotten all about me.

"Both of them had forgotten about me.

"I stood there, neither dead nor alive.

"Perhaps my breath stopped, too. Just my eyes went from one to the other.

"Finally, Bloody Eye saw me. He seemed amazed to see me, couldn't figure out why I was there. Then he must have remembered. And I read it on his face: Get lost! I don't remember whether he actually said it aloud, but I lowered my head, opened the door very carefully, and went out quietly—very quietly, as if I hadn't been there in the first place. It was only in the street, when the cold struck, that I came to my senses.

"After that, I wasn't summoned to translate. And I didn't know what happened in the farmhouse. What did Sam-iki say to Bloody Eye when they were alone? Nobody on the River— neither kith nor kin—ever knew. It remains a mystery to this day, lost in darkness."

From CHAPTER 21

Demyan lived with the memory of the happiness he had known while traveling with the wonderful and exciting Marina.

It was raining, drizzling. And their talk was like the rain—even and slow.

"Isn't it boring in the woods?" the girl asked.

"Life, you mean?"

"Everything . . ."

"No, it's much worse in the settlement. Everyone says so—those who live on their own land, those in the villages."

"Why?"

"There's no time to be bored in the woods. You have to keep busy. If you don't, you wouldn't survive."

"There's that much work?"

"Not work, perhaps, but *concerns*. Many concerns."

"Such as?"

"Well, different things. Things you do in the spring, for instance. Things you do in summer. Then autumn. Then winter. Each season brings its own concerns . . ."

Demyan paused. "Hunting and fishing and deer pasturing—that's obvious. It goes on year round. What else? In the spring you make canoes and boats for summer. It's also the time for hunting geese and ducks. In summer you fish. Get clay for the *chuvals,* the storage sheds. Store birch bark and cedar roots. The birch bark's for roofing; the roots are for basketry. You also make various tools out of cedar, pine, fir, birch, and the cherry nut tree. You need all kinds of trees.

"Toward fall you start making sledges, weave *mordas*—fishnets—and prepare snares. Then you clean the spots on the rivers where you'll put out the nets. Later, when the gnats are gone, you start to build new houses and sheds and to repair the old ones. And in winter, there's no time for a break! The days are short—just right for hunting. You start at dawn and return at dusk, when you can no longer see your gun barrel. You start and return in darkness.

"These are a man's occupations. But a woman has many chores, too, perhaps more. The woman is in charge of house-keeping, of clothing, shoes, of taking care of the children. When a family loses its housekeeper, we say *the fire is out in that hearth*. And it's right that we say so. Everything is in her hands. And the woodland villagers have many other chores— morning chores, afternoon chores, evening chores. There's no time for boredom," Demyan concluded.

"Why is it worse in town? Life's easier, there are fewer . . . concerns."

"No. In the big towns and settlements our people have no survival skills."

"None? Do they need any?"

"Of course. In the woods, in his own village, a man does something every day. He has things to do. In town, he loses these tasks. When he finishes his daily job, he goes home, and there's nothing for him to do."

"Isn't that good? More free time, more time for rest?"

"No-o," Demyan insisted. "He mustn't have free time. Our people haven't developed the habit of leisure."

"Why not?"

"If you've nothing to do, you start drinking wine and vodka. Begin drinking, and you're soon gone . . . . If you have no money to buy a drink, you go to the house of a neighbor or relative— anybody's. They'll always pour you a drink. It's our custom."

"How do you know?"

"I've seen it. The settlement is small. We know a lot about each other."

"But couldn't they still do something in town, in their free time?"

"What would they do? They've no need for sledges or ca-noes. Fishnets and snares are out, too."

"What about hunting?"

"Where? The family hunting grounds are far away. If you work, everything must be near. Those who live in town a long time eventually lose their hunting skills. They lose interest in the woods, in woodcraft."

"I see," the girl mused.

The rain continued. They were silent, their thoughts imitating the quiet talk of the skies.

"What about holidays?" she asked. "Say, the New Year?"

"In the woods they don't celebrate the New Year. It's the wrong kind of holiday."

"Why?" The girl was amazed.

"Tell me—are New Year's trees put in every home?"

"Almost in everyone's."

"Same as in the towns?"

"The same."

"And are there fir trees everywhere?"

"Fir trees, yes."

"Think, now. Is it worth it—all over the world—for the sake of one day, to kill so many live trees? Do we really need to?"

"Well . . ." The girl hesitated. "I'd have to think about that."

"People think there's no need," Demyan said. "And I think they're right. Once, after New Year's Day, I went to the settlement, and there were used fir trees almost everywhere—broken, as bare as skeletons. Dead. That's when it occurred to me—there's no need to kill so many trees for the sake of a single day!"

"But surely we need decorations for the holiday."

"Of course. But within reason. With us, for example, each clan has a Sacred Tree. They're in the Sacred Groves, on the Sacred Hills. When people go there, they adorn the trees with cloth or hides, so the Tree won't die but will live for many years."

"But the New Year is a religious holiday, to worship God!"

"Worship?" Demyan said. "That depends on how you define it. The custom's the same, though. Our elders say that *you* have your New Year's tree, *we* have our Sacred Tree. You adorn it, and so do we. You wish each other health, prosperity, happiness, and good luck. And so do we. It's the same holiday with a different emphasis. If God exists, he sees both your New Year's tree and our Sacred Tree. If God doesn't exist, he sees neither, right? There's just one difference—you worship a dead tree, while we worship a living one. I think our way reflects the nature of human life. The elders say that after your worship, the tree dies. After ours, it continues to live. Isn't that reasonable? Aren't they right?"

"Many aspects of our life don't make sense," the girl said. "Perhaps everyone is right in his own way."

The fire was almost out. Demyan stood up and added more firewood. The wet boughs hissed on the coals and gave off thick smoke. The mosquitoes won't like it, he thought. Good smoke.

"What about birthdays?" the girl asked.

"Only for children. Before they're three or four. Some continue until five or six."

"And then?"

"They forget them entirely."

"How do they know their age, then?"

"There are several ways. For example, we count the years between certain events that all the people along the River remember. Say, the Year of Big Water, the Year When the Reds Came, the Year of the Wood Fires, and so on. You can calculate your birthday from these events. Another way is to compare your own age with that of someone older or younger."

"Why don't the adults observe birthdays?"

"Perhaps it isn't tactful to remind a man, with each passing year, that he is closer and closer to old age. What kind of a holiday is that, especially for the old ones?"

"That's reasonable," the girl smiled. "Stop counting between eighteen and twenty, and then—eternal youth! No need to count anything!"

"Right," Demyan nodded. "Why count?"

"So it looks like there weren't many holidays?"

"No, no! They say there were many in the old days. Now there are fewer and fewer each year."

"What other holidays did your people celebrate?"

"The biggest and merriest was the Bear Dance. In our village they danced the Bear often. He was a frequent guest. My father would call him out of the woods, a roundabout way of saying 'to kill a bear.' Then Uncle Vasil and my godfather Yefrem the Elder and many of my relatives and kinsmen would dance."

"Who presided over the feast—the shaman?"

"The shaman? Who told you that?" Demyan shook his head. "The shaman had other things to do. If he didn't know the myth-songs, there was no use for him. He could be present, of course, but just as another guest."

"Who was in charge, then?"

"The main figure at a Bear Dance is the singer."

"Are there many?"

"Well, everyone sings, but not all songs are good for the Bear Dance. Special myth-songs are needed. Each has its own theme. They're sung with a special mythic quality in the voice. The great singers have this quality. We have singers in our family, too. Yefim Andreevich, my blood brother, for one. They call him the Gray Hair. His father, Andrew the Elder, is a singer, too. I heard them at the feast when I was a child. They can sing for two whole days—there's no end to the myths they know. We passed their village earlier. And Ivan Petrovich, who lives downriver, is another. They call him the Proud Pipe because he takes his pipe with him everywhere. My uncle, from my own clan, is a great singer, too. None of them is a shaman—I know that for sure. And my godfather Yefrem the Elder sings, too. He knows all the myth-songs of the Bear Feast.

"Leykov Joseph lives in the next village on our way. He's a

relative, although his name is different. He's a singer, too. As they say in these parts, *he has a very good throat*—his singing can put you to sleep. I've never heard anyone with a voice like his. There are none like him on the River.

"When we get to his village you'll see a long and sandy stretch of land on the right bank of the River. There's a good pine grove with *yagel*-moss on top. They have their spring and autumn village over there, and their pasture. Their summer village is across the River, on a broad white sandy beach. We'll stop at the big plank house there. It overlooks the River. We'll stop for tea, to look around. . . . Further on, a little ways down the mouth of the Vat-Yegan, the River's right tributary, there's a village of Yepi and Kochp-iki brothers. They're also singers and kinsmen of mine."

"Your kinsmen live everywhere! You have so many!" The girl was amazed. "You've invaded the entire River!"

"We haven't invaded anything. We live here," Demyan said. "And not along the entire River, just the middle part."

He was silent a while and then admitted that his clan, indeed, was perhaps the most populous on the River. It was split into two groups—the Marsh People and the River People. His own village was among the Marsh People, the rest were in the River group, the ones who had lived at the mouth of the Vat-Yegan since the old days. They were called the Ust-Vat-Yegan People and were mostly fisherman, while the Marsh People were reindeer breeders.

"And there are singers in every clan," Demyan said thoughtfully. "Further down river, in the Moose clan of the Mohtic-Yegan village, there's a great singer—Pokachev Grigori the Elder. He knows so many myths he can dance the Bear alone. Other great singers exist only in memory—Nerm-Iki, the father of the postman Galaktion, whose Russian name was Stepan the Elder. Few ever heard him sing—he died young."

Then Demyan told the girl about the house where they kept

the bones of the Bear—every last one. It was made of logs, and it was raised a little higher than a man, so the beasts couldn't get into it. The top was covered with a layer of smaller logs. After the feast, they put the Bear's things there—the *kujenki,* or vessels; the masks, the little walking sticks, the little planks for His "house," and so on. The log house stands on one or two legs, usually a thick tree trunk sawed off at just the right height. Everything about the log house is done neatly.

"I've heard a lot about the Bear Feast," the girl said. "But I've never seen it. How does it go?"

"O-oh, it's impossible to put into words," Demyan said. "You must see and hear it for yourself. Just once in your life. When you describe it, you spoil it—distort it."

"Still," the girl insisted, "I'd like to know . . ."

Demyan checked the fire. Then, straightening up, he looked over the low cloudy sky and, as if convinced that the rain wouldn't end soon—that there was no reason to hurry—began telling about the Bear Dance.

"The ritual starts when the beast is called from the forest— someone outside the village dresses in the ritual bearskin. They pretend to unbutton his coat and take it off. Then he is brought to the village. As they near the houses they stop and shoot into the sky five times. If it is a She-Bear they shoot four times. This is the signal to the villagers to get ready to meet their Black-Faced Guest, to quickly put on their shoes. By no means should you show Him your bare feet. That would be disrespectful.

"When the Bear arrives, the entire village comes to meet Him, to greet Him, to kiss Him on the nose. Then, in order to amuse Him and make Him happy, they pour water on some-one, or someone will wrestle an opponent in a test of strength. Later, when the hunters have rested from preparing the birch bark masks, the little walking sticks, the rectangular block of cedar wood, and the little planks for the Bear's 'house,' they lead Him into the home of the host hunter—not through the front door but through the rooftop, the purest entrance. Everything must be very clean. And the Bear is greeted with a shout—*Chovie-chovie!*—repeated three times.

"What does it mean?" Demyan said. "There's no way to translate. It must be some ancient spell. Then the Bear is seated, and they position His head and front paws. Behind Him, in a vessel covered with hide and clothing, they put His heart, His backbone, and other main parts. All these are named indirectly. If you don't know the language, you won't understand anything. For example, you can never say *dogs* in the same breath with His name. This would hurt His feelings. So they refer to them as *the tailed ones.*

"Then they make Him a house—two walls of five planks on the left and right, intersected horizontally by five more to form a bunk, with open space for the 'windows.' For a She-Bear they use four planks in each part. Then the house is ready. Next they put a rectangular block of cedar by His right paw. This represents a small cedar tree. It's about waist high and extends just above the walls of His house. A cord is tied to the trunk of this 'cedar tree' and fastened with a little bell for the myth-songs. Right by the tip of His nose they thrust an arrow-like rod. To the right sits an oven and a wooden poker. These are real, as are the flint and steel for striking the fire. The Bear's 'comb' is made of wood. For eyes—His 'stars'—they affix two big bright metal buttons, which gleam as if He is watching everything. But these eyes are immediately covered by a cap—by a kerchief if it is a She-Bear, while Her paws are adorned with rings, beads, and chains. They say the She-Bear likes beautiful jewelry.

"Then they put a table before the Bear, set with a tea mug and three small *kujenkas* with food. All four corners of these vessels are bent to the right, toward the sun. Then the Bear is led into His house, is seated, and the main part of the feast begins. But with His eyes covered, the Bear sleeps on his bunk. So the best singer, usually a respected elder, awakens Him with the little bell, then performs the myth called *Kyingem-Yeingem*. The singer wears a birch bark mask and lays the little walking stick across his knees. This myth-song is long—about forty minutes—and toward the end, when the singer comes to the words 'left star open, right star open,' the cap is pulled away and the Bear can see everything.

"Then the host hunter lights the fire with his flint and steel and tends the coals in the stove. We believe, of course, that the Bear does all this Himself. Then the host hunter combs His hair and paws with the wooden comb and cleans Him up. Then everyone greets Him, kissing His paws or nose. Small children are brought to Him. Then the host takes a cup of water, turns toward the sun in a circle three times, and with the words '*Choviechovie!*' sprinkles water on the walls and people. He pours the rest of the water over some young hunter and instantly they start to wrestle. If the host wins, he must take on another opponent, and yet another, until he is defeated. Encouraging the wrestlers, the elders used to cry, 'Put the host by his Bear!' And eventually, with no time to rest, the weary host is pinned to the ground.

"Games and jokes follow. Someone might pour water on you, but you mustn't take offense. Such pranks are only played among those who are on joking terms—among brothers and their sister-in-law, for example, or a husband's younger brother. But among those who habitually avoid each other, joking's impossible at the Bear Dance. And who does this include? A father and his daughter-in-law, a mother and her son-in-law, a mother-in-law and her husband's elder brothers, a father and his son-in-law. Everything must stay within the bounds of politeness. And there are games, jokes, and merriment for the Bear Himself. The singer enters the house, wearing a birch bark mask, gloves, and carrying a walking stick. He greets everyone—'*Pechapecha!*'—then asks:

" 'Whose house is this? Why are so many people here?'

"And they answer:

" 'This is the Bear's house. We have come here together.'

" 'The Bear's house? That's just where I was going myself!'

"And they ask him:

" 'Perhaps you have some myth-songs to share?'

" 'Oh, a few,' he answers. 'Do you really want to hear them?'

" 'Yes, yes,' they say. 'Can you remember one or two?'

" 'Well, if you need them, I do remember one. I guess I'll begin.'

"With this the singer stands in front of the Bear, or he may sit, greeting Him once more—'*Pecha-pecha!*'—and begins to sing. Throughout the performance he turns his head to the left and right, sending the song in different directions, into unmeasured distances, toward every man and woman. Everybody sits and listens attentively. When the song is over, the singer says '*Shen toty ngenty.*' And what does that mean? Again, no translation exists. The words must be very old. Each myth begins with *Pecha-pecha!* and ends with *Shen toty ngenty.*

"Later, two more obligatory myths are performed and various shorter pieces follow—myth-songs, dances, scenes, a free-for-all. Children may sing or dance, too, or act out a piece. There is more wrestling, more games and jokes. Usually these satirize avarice, laziness, cowardice, and other human vices. Sometimes they touch on people present. But you can't take offense—all this supposedly comes from the Bear. How can you take offense with the Bear?

"This continues until the singers grow tired and need a break. Then one of the singers puts the Bear to sleep, performing *Kyingem-Yeingem* with the little bell. At the words 'left star open, right star open' they put the cap over His eyes and He is asleep. The first day of the Bear Dance is over. The singers rest—drink tea, smoke pipes—and tend to their daily affairs.

"Then a bit of wood is chipped from the upper two vertical planks of Bear's house to signify the first day of the feast, and to the Bear's right they put a four-sided marking block on which

is carved the number of the feast and various objects of importance—bows, arrows, arrowheads, ornaments, and mysterious
designs. The myth-songs are also counted by cuts on the block.

"Then the Bear's food is cleared away and eaten. People like
to eat from the Bear's table—it's supposed to bring good luck.
On the second day they'll bring fresh tea and food.

"And after everyone is rested, the second day of the feast
begins, when the singer awakens the Bear with the little bell.
As on the first day, short myth-songs follow, then acted scenes,
music, dancing, and wrestling. Then comes the third day, and
the myths become more complicated, or perhaps more serious.
First the singers address the spirits of *urmans,* the local gods.
On all rivers and clan grounds are places where these *urman*
gods have lived. Then the singers perform myths of the regional
and main gods. These are the principal myths, the sacred ones.
They're obligatory, and if no singer is present who knows them
from beginning to end, the Bear Dance cannot be completed.

"These sacred myths are performed in a set sequence, until
the fifth day of the feast. What are they all about? Life, obviously. They recount the story of humanity on Earth, the entire
story of the Khanty people—how the Earth was created, and
the people on it, the Sun and Moon, the Stars and the Milky
Way, the birds and beasts, the waters and woods, the Upper
and Lower Worlds. They tell, too, how the Bear came to Earth,
and what happened in the Lower World, and about life in the
Upper and Middle Worlds during times of love and hate, war
and peace, triumph and defeat. They tell how people came to
the brink of extinction during the world calamity of the Great
Waters. The myths sing and tell about all of this, as well as
many other things, and it is all sung and told to the Bear, who
is our guest.

"Toward the end of the Dance longer pieces are acted out,
such as the appearance of the Owl. Then comes the archery
and wrestling. This is always exciting. Then the shooting of ar-

rows over the six-legged Moose. Everyone's fascinated by this, too. Then comes the Heath-Cock dance, and the Milking of the Cows dance. Many people participate, and everyone is welcome to play and dance.

"The fifth day of the feast is the final one. Only a kettle with *kasha,* a kind of gruel, sits on the Bear's table, and a ring is thrown in. Later, when everyone eats, the luckiest person will get the ring. But it's customary for whoever gets it not to mention it.

"The feast continues until it's time for the *Torh,* or Crane, myth. One singer performs it to the sound of the bell, while another covers himself with a big kerchief and acts the part of the Crane.

"Spring has come, and the Crane—or She-Crane, rather—is back from the South. She settles upon her native marsh and rejoices in eating some of last year's cranberries. She makes a nest and lays three eggs. She sings and dances happily. Then the Fox comes. As soon as the Crane leaves the nest, the Fox steals one of her eggs. When the Crane returns, she sees one egg missing—one of her children—and she goes crazy from grief and anger. She throws one of the eggs over her right wing to her Sky Father, the Supreme God *Numi Torum,* stomping the other egg into the ground for the Earth Mother. Then, spreading her wings, she flies away. And as she flies, she sees the house where the Bear Dance is being held, where the Bear is sitting. And the mad Crane attacks the Bear's house, scattering all the little planks, breaking the walking sticks, tearing up the masks. With her sharp beak she pierces the birch bark dishes, making holes in them, then flies away, crying *'Curriv-riv!'* What can you do with a Crane crazed by anger and grief?

"'*Shen toty ngenty,*' the singer ends, and the little bell is silent.

"After such devastation, all is sad and quiet in the house.

"Then, starting at the Bear's head, the men file out, from

one side of the house all the way to the door, holding each other by their little fingers. The women do the same, from the other side of the house. They make a narrow path to the half-open door, and the last pair—a man and woman—take the Bear by the 'little fingers' attached to his house on the right and left. Then the singer begins the final myth, Seeing the Bear's Soul Out, or Bidding Farewell to the Bear in the Taiga. The parting melody is sad. Everyone listens in silence. What does it say? That the angry Crane has destroyed the Bear's house, has broken His possessions, and that now, since He is homeless, He must go back into the taiga forest, into His *urman* grounds and woods. His Soul, through the narrow path of men and women, must return to the taiga. And there, when the time comes, it will turn into the Bear again.

"That's the whole idea of the feast—to return the Bear to nature. He is called from the forest, but with the help of the ritual, He is returned to His *urmans,* to His domain. He does not vanish. He lives forever on Earth, and the singers are there to remember his sacred myths . . . .

"And that," Demyan sighed, "is how the Bear Dance ends."

The girl was silent, lost in thought, staring into the fire.

It was still raining. It seemed you could hear the drops flow over the trees into the ground of the taiga. There was no end to the heavenly flow.

Demyan checked the fire, and Marina, back from her thoughts, looked at him, barely smiling with her spring-like marshy eyes. Then she said quietly:

"I wish someone would return my soul to nature." And raising her hands, she ran her fingers through her hair. Then, slowly, palms open, her slim fingers trembling, she ran them through the leaves of the nearest autumn larch tree.

And at that moment, spellbound by the spring-like light in her eyes, Demyan suddenly understood that she was already in nature, all of her, on his Earth. And he knew his Earth well and loved it with a strong and silent love that they would never reveal to anyone, ever. And because of that she grew closer, like one of his own kin, understanding him better.

He didn't know then that this memory of her would torment him at every spring marsh, at every autumn larch, at every bend of the lake and river. She would surround him in the days and years to come—in the flowers, in the woodland sounds. In the shadows of his taiga forest, his Earth.

AND SO DIES MY CLAN

I speak to you from the Lower World. I am a shadow, a phantom. A ghost. I am here, and yet I am not. You hear me, and yet you don't. Why? Because this year I turned forty. And like many clansmen and relatives of the same age, I've already been to the Lower World. Once, twice, even three times—I have died. Why? Why have we gone to the Other World before our time? Because we've lost our life-space. There is no place left for us on this earth. No place to live, to breathe, to feel joy and sorrow.

Our ancestral land is gone. My seventy-eight-year-old father understood this long ago, when no one yet believed in the end of the land—in the end of clan and tribe. Perhaps he understood it for the first time that evening in January when, on an empty winter road, his way was suddenly blocked by a truck that had stopped ahead of him. His reindeer team stopped, too, for there was nowhere to go. Two men got out of the truck and came up to the sledge. One grasped the old man from behind, while the other removed his native fur boots—his *kisi*. Then they leisurely returned to their truck and drove away. My father came home in his socks, glad they hadn't touched his deer. Glad he wasn't too far from home. That he didn't freeze.

This happened in the year that the oilmen, conquering "virgin territory," cut a winter road through the forest of our clan, from Nizhnevartovsk to their base settlement at New Agansk. And my father began taking that road to get his pension check every month. From that day on, he began to mark the passage of time differently. Whenever he spoke, he would point out that such and such an event had taken place that winter, when they took his *kisi*. Or that autumn, when a motorboat broke open the storage house in his summer camp and his fur clothing was stolen. Events like these, during the course of twenty or thirty years, were more than enough.

One winter, in his logging camp, his best reindeer team was gone.

In berry season a helicopter landed near the autumn village and made off with all the deer hides and raw materials for winter clothing and boots. Then a drilling station appeared on the Sacred Hill and desecrated the area with filth and refuse. And the state clear-cutting agency felled trees at the clan cemetery, devastating our eternal resting-place.

And there was more, much more than my father, the hunter, could comprehend in a lifetime. For in all of his seventy-eight years he had never touched a single pine needle, leaf, or blade of grass on his land or clan grounds without a grave need. He couldn't understand why forests that harbor the white moss— the *yagel* so loved by the deer—were cut down. Why forests were turned into logs left to rot in unwanted piles. Why drilling teams left behind them upturned soil, heaps of iron, plank houses, and dead pines. Why machines, with their iron pipes and sand, so strangled the necks of the little rivers that neither fish nor fishermen could get through. Why they pumped oil— the burning fat of the earth—so it floated along the Agan River three fingers thick, killing everything in its wake. Floated for weeks. It would be good to clean it, but how? It would be good to return it to the belly of the earth. But how?

Why? Where? How? These questions still torment my father. Who can answer them? The ministries and institutions? They're too far away, my father thinks. Farther than God himself. For if *Numi Torum,* the supreme god of the Khanty people, listens to their prayers only sometimes, these men never will. But if you believe in rumor, good men who *will* listen *do* exist somewhere on this earth.

The land is gone. And my father finds himself trapped,

surrounded. To the west, down the Agan River, is the town of Pokachi, where Pokachi Oil—the oil-drilling department—is boss. To the north lies the city of Kogalym and, a little closer, the Povhov oil site. To the east, toward the headwaters of the Agan, live the geologists of New Agansk and the city of Radujnii, where the Varyogan Oil & Gas Company is the oil-processing boss. And to the south, beyond the clan's native *urmans*, lies the main, huge oil deposit at Samotlor. Besides that, the local logging farm snatches whatever's nearest and easiest and casts the rest to the wind.

I ask my father, "What do you need? How can I help?"

After a long silence, he says: "Nothing. Just give me land. Some land where I can pasture the deer, hunt, and fish. Give me some land where my deer would be safe from the teeth of stray dogs, where my hunting paths won't be trampled by poachers and machines, where the black fat of the earth doesn't flow over lakes and rivers. I need land where my own house, my sacred site and resting-place, would be safe. I need land where I won't be robbed of my clothing and boots in broad daylight. Not someone else's land, but my own. Just a little patch, a tiny speck, of my own."

How can I answer that? *Who* could answer that?

If my father wants his own land, why not grant his wish?

Who's for it? And who's against?

Well, plenty are against it, and they'll prevail. They'll utter pretty words and be supportive, but when they get down to business there'll be thousands of reasons why my father can't have his own land. He'll never live to see it.

Land is the major stumbling block.

The land of our ancestors is gone. And gone is our clan, the kin of Maha the Beaver, who once settled the middle region of the Agan River, tributary to the Ob, between the oil cities of Surgut and Nizhnevartovsk. As I understand it now, the clan died from a sense of hopelessness, a sense of doom. By the age of forty, before their time, almost all of my cousins and second cousins perished from alcohol.

Aipin Yefim fell from a boat and drowned.

Aipin Galaktion drowned, returning from the settlement during a thaw.

Aipin Nikita fell from a motorboat and drowned.

Aipin Dmitri fell from a motorboat and drowned.

Aipin Aisir, returning from the settlement, froze on the road. Then his wife, with her deer team, on the same winter road, was killed by a truck. Aipin Anton fell into the river from a dock and drowned.

Aipin Maxim, at the age of seventeen, was shot point blank by a drunken logger, a newcomer in town.

Leikov Galaktion fell from a boat and drowned.

Leikov Leonid fell from a boat and drowned.

My uncle Aipin Vassili Efremovich fell asleep in a drunken stupor and never woke up.

Aipin Mikhail fell asleep in a drunken stupor and never woke up.

All of them, except Maxim, had families and children. What happened to them? They became nobodies. Families without fathers came to live in the settlements and towns. There was no one to teach the boys how to hunt, how to make snares, fishnets, sledges, and boats. How to build homes and storage houses. They had missed what their fathers and grandfathers learned from childhood. So they couldn't become hunters or fishermen or deer breeders. Nor did they make "the great leap from tribalism to socialism," as all the sociologists proclaimed. None of them became oilmen, or geologists, or builders. Why? Because most of them never were schooled beyond the eighth grade. They remained uneducated and therefore unwanted—in the village, the city, the taiga, the oil business.

And what about the girls? Their fate was even more dramatic. They lost that thing without which no nation can continue:

they never became wives, mothers, and hearthkeepers. They never learned how to sew fur clothing or make boots. They never learned how to process hides, to work with birch bark, pine bark, or cedar roots. To make clay ovens and bake bread. To process smoked or dried fish and meat for storage. They never grasped the wonderful world of native ornament, which from the earliest of times has adorned the clothing of Khanty girls. What did they get instead? Nothing. No education. What did they do? There was a demand for them, all right. Never getting beyond the eighth grade, they were abused by the men in the nearest industrial towns and cities. Where the main population is men, there's always a demand for women.

Torn from the land.

Contaminated by vodka and wine.

Corrupted.

Severed from the root that binds a people to its land.

And this is how my nieces and nephews swelled the ranks of an army of tramps. Unemployed, living by chance, drinking, and wasting away their lives. In my village of Varyogan, in the Nizhnevartovsk district, not far from the famous Samotlor, the number employed at the local state industries—including Russians, Tartars, and Ukrainians—is sixty-seven people. And the unemployed—natives all—number fifty-three. The figures are for 1986.

The unemployed in Varyogan include ten of my clansmen who bear the name of Aipin. Many of them want to work, but there is no work. There is only the local sawmill. All positions that involve manual labor, as precious as gold, were taken long ago—at the boarding school, first aid clinic, the local store, and other village agencies.

And yet, not so long ago, the village was busy, working as a collective farm. Besides hunting and fishing, the locals pastured three reindeer herds. They had thirty head of cattle, ten horses, and they raised polar foxes. They planted potatoes and other vegetables. But later, with the coming of the oil industry and the turmoil that followed, all that was gone. And the people who loved the land were gone, too.

This is how my nieces and nephews became a lost generation, with no knowledge of their native language or culture. This is how the clan of Maha the Beaver—my clan—went the way of the setting sun. One more step, and the entire clan will be there, beyond the horizon, with no chance of return.

But even there, beyond that magic black line, there's no peace for the dead. Out of sheer greed, those who conquered this virgin territory have plundered the grave of my uncle, Aipin Nikolai, at a village near New Agansk. A while later, in the same place, they plundered the grave of my other uncle, Aipin Peter. Nor did they leave in peace my third uncle, Aipin Yefim, the storyteller and singer, who died in February 1984. He too was thrown from his grave near his ancestral Sacred Hill.

Who are they, these intruders into the dust of the grave? How did they ever come to live on this earth? Shall the dead never rest? It seems so, for a man no longer belongs to his land, to his clan, or to himself. Or to the spirit world. And the desecrators continue their black deeds because nothing can stop them. Not even the police, who are still looking for the thieves who robbed my father. Responding to complaints of the people, the police keep saying that they have other, more urgent business to attend to. Which is true to an extent. There are many more serious crimes in the area.

At first I naively thought that, with the discovery of oil, all the misfortunes were my father's alone. But later I realized it was otherwise. Others suffered, too, some more, some less. Along the Agan River all the ancient Khanty clans—the Pokachevs, Tyrlins, Sardakovs, Kazamkins, Tilchins, as well as the Nenets clans of Iusi and Aivaseda—are in the same boat. All suffered the same losses. All have the same pains.

Considering their standard of living, how do they exist?

In June 1988, I saw the Native village of Agan. Here, in a Nizhnevartovsk fish-processing factory, the minimum salary for a Native woman is thirteen rubles. A month. And all of the work is heavy labor—loading and unloading, salting and processing. And there's not a single piece of machinery to help.

Not to mention the living conditions. The wooden houses, which were built in the Native villages following the state decree of 1955, have rotted through and through. Yet many families still manage to somehow live in them. There's nowhere else to go.

And these conditions exist right next door to the gold-mining industry of Samotlor, where the smokestacks have already burned for decades above such human poverty. Under the old system, the local Soviets and other agencies had to scavenge every nail from the all-powerful oil companies in order to survive in the Native villages. And now, after Russia's conversion to a market economy, even the nails will be out of reach.

And far from Samotlor the situation is also serious. I've seen it myself. For the Khanty people on the rivers Vah, Tromagan, Kazym, Yugan, Pim, Lyamin, and Nazym—as with the Mansi people on the Sosva and Kanda—it's the same as on the Agan, the same as among my kin, with little variation. Everywhere there is but one issue—the land! Where to raise the deer, to hunt and fish, where to gather berries and mushrooms.

The Pim Khanty near the Surgut have it the worst. They are besieged on all sides by oil sites and drilling units. They are being driven from their native grounds, rushing between drilling stations, oil pipes, and concrete highways with their families and possessions in tow. They spend both winter and summer in ragged tents. Stray dogs and poachers have destroyed all their deer, and game and fish have become scarce. The land itself is gone. Lyantor Oil finally decided to build the Pim a village near the industrial town of Lyantor, in a swamp fortified by sand. The people themselves requested a site twenty miles away, near the middle of the Pim River. There is good pinewood there, and most important, it is closer to their hunting and fishing grounds, to the deer food—the *yagel* moss—and to berries and mushrooms. This is crucial for the elderly, for the women and children, so there's no problem with transportation. But this spring the Pim were issued an ultimatum—either go live by Lyantor or do without a village. At Lyantor, the oil people argued, it's easier to connect the village to electricity, heating, water, and roads.

And so they began construction work on that swamp.

Yet nobody worries about the fact that in a decade or two all the Pim Khanty will be gone. Which will be good for the oilmen who take their lands. But we've already experienced the bitter policy of terminating "unpromising villages." That campaign in our region is a national disaster. All who were torn from the land—from their traditional economy in the heart of their hunting grounds—and brought into the towns have basically become drunks, losing their material and spiritual culture in the process. And so the next generation grew up without its Native language, rejecting any relationship to the past of its own people. This was the lost generation of my nieces and nephews on the Agan River.

It will be a pity if the Pim Khanty die out, with their unique folklore, folk art, and language. They differ from the Agan, or Vah, or any other Khanty people. They're a separate ethnic group numbering only four hundred. They won't be able to hold their own against the oil giants. For one thing, they're all illiterate. Four years ago I didn't meet a single Native person there who had even made it to the eighth grade. Most had only two or three years of boarding school, rarely five or six grades.

The Pim land is also at its end, ready to disappear. Yet we would like to see the Pim Khanty live, for the world culture will be poorer without them. Is there no way to save them?

And what about the Tromagan Khanty? They're not so

much better off. A local "developer" was recently brought by helicopter from an old drilling station with an arrow stuck in his behind. One old hunter, tired of thieves, had put a crossbow in his storage hut, and the daredevil adventurer, looking for easy spoils, got what was coming to him. He wanted the arrow removed, but it was an arrow meant for an otter, with harp hooks, so they had to fly him to Surgut for an operation.

But they couldn't save another fellow adventurer who took a bullet from the Elder of the Nenets camp at Alta. Yet in court, to the amazement of the Natives, nobody questioned what business this guy had in a Nenets camp during working hours, in a state car with a state driver and plenty of moonshine. Yet the question was crucial for the Natives because their future depended on it: would alcohol be allowed into the camp? A few months later the Elder died in prison in Tobolsk.

My relatives from the Yugan River, who are just beginning to experience the oil problem, are luckier. Here's what they write to me:

"The various 'conquerors of virgin territory' break into the hunting huts on our native grounds and take whatever items they like. Boats and motors, our basic necessities, disappear. And from year to year it is becoming more difficult to preserve our cemeteries.

"We protest the destruction of the natural environment in our area, which is turning into our own destruction. We understand that the country needs oil, but not at the expense of our lives! All local industrial works operate as if we weren't here, as if our ancestors weren't here, as if our existence were over. Where are the principles of government policy toward Native peoples?

"We sincerely ask the government to save our small people while it's still possible, to leave us the lands along the Big Yugan and Little Yugan Rivers, to ease all oil drilling there, and all construction beyond the village of Ugut. Let us proclaim this region an eco-zone. The Khanty expect that the government will recognize our problems among its global concerns and take real steps to preserve the Native peoples."

This official letter, sent in 1988 by the fishermen and hunters of the Ugut division of the Surgut cooperative farm, bore one hundred signatures. It could just as well have been signed by all twenty-one thousand of the Khanty people and all those who still have a conscience.

But the barbarous exploitation of the land continues. In West Siberia alone, more than 100 million acres of deer pastures have been destroyed. Twenty-eight rivers, with 170,000 acres of spawning grounds, are contaminated by oil. Half of the gas extracted is burned right into the atmosphere. Hundreds of accidents have occurred in each of the companies.

What's more valuable, an extra ton of oil or the fate of a human being? A ton of oil or the fate of an entire people? Can this barbarity be stopped?

Of course not. The machine that is crawling over the lands of the Natives of the North is too heavy and too poorly managed. What has been lost in recent years is irretrievable.

Is there any way out for my people?

Yes, there is. We must preserve the lands that are still unmolested. For this to happen, we have to create, by government decree, national park zones in the areas traditionally inhabited by Native peoples. The national economy wouldn't suffer much, for if the industrial policy is reasonable, the natural resources will last for centuries just by using the existing sites.

It doesn't matter what we call these native territories—national parks, reserves, or autonomous regions. The main thing is that they must exist. Today. *Now.* Or there'll be no more need for them decades from now, because no one will be interested.

Reserve territories could solve many current problems. First, the Native language could be preserved in its own milieu. It's easier to learn your own language from your mother than from textbooks. The latter don't exist, anyway. Second, the traditional economy—hunting, fishing, and the raising of deer—would form the basis of the material culture. And third, reserve territories would ensure the health of the people. Fresh fish and meat, berries and mushrooms can physically preserve the people better than spaghetti and canned food, at thirteen rubles a month, in the cities.

Without such territories, people will lose their spirituality, people known for their music, songs, dances, and folk epics. The Bear Feasts of the people of the North involve all aspects of the folk arts, some aspects of which have been recorded by Hungarian and Finnish scholars since the last century. Yet under the pressure of the oil invasion, the last guardians of the spiritual and material traditions are dying out.

An oil tank can be replenished, but the soul of a people— never!

Each time my father passes by the desecrated Sacred Hill he murmurs in prayer:

O Gods, free my land from oil.
O Gods, deliver my land into my own hands.

Will his prayers be heard on Earth or in Heaven?

We need specialists who know the Native languages, yet it's difficult to produce them, for half of the villages in the Surgut area don't even have schools. Children can only be raised properly in the family, by parents, so schools must be brought closer to the hunting and fishing villages. Why can the Norwegians, for example, open schools for as few as five pupils, but we cannot? Instead, we drag the children across many miles to boarding schools. We need teachers who would migrate with the deer herds and teach the children in the nearby villages. Otherwise, all will remain as before, just laws on paper.

Native areas deserve special consideration from the administrative agencies. Most of all, we need a system that guarantees *self-government* in our own territories.

If everything continues as it is now, my kinsman will not only get nothing, but they will also lose the last of what they still have. They will not even have six feet of earth for burial, to go decently to the Lower World.

I am a ghost. I do not exist. Because the statistics say that my relatives die many times before their deaths.

Can you imagine how this feels? Trying to breathe with our children in this atmosphere of doom? If you can, then you understand me and my departed relatives, who were eager to drink anything that would help them escape from reality, even for a moment.

As for me, I defy the logic of statistics that say, "You must go. You must leave this Earth soon!" I don't want to believe in the end of my clan. The end of this Earth, and the end of my people.

That is why I take my pen and write this down.

Nadezda Taligina (KHANTY)

(

Nadezda Taligina, born in 1953, is a Khanty artist and scholar coming from the family of a reindeer breeder. After graduating from the Salekhard Cultural Studies College, she studied in Moscow at the Stroganov School of Art from 1982 to 1987, specializing in jewelry. She spent the year of 1992 in the Academic Center for the Study of Northern Native Cultures of the Yamal-Nenets autonomous area, then applied for postgraduate work at the University of Tomsk, West Siberia, in order to be able to teach Native children the differences between traditional and academic visual arts.

"When I drew the everyday life of the Khanty," she has said, "I couldn't understand myself what I was seeing. I needed time to figure it out." Thus began her study of local Native cultures, resulting in black-and-white drawings (as in the following portfolio) that are known throughout Siberia.

Taligina works frequently as a book illustrator. Her style combines ethnologic precision and lyricism. In the pieces that follow, one should note the difference between the "black" and the "transparent" figures, the latter being visionary and idealized, existing only in the perception of real persons.

Taligina and her husband live in Salekhard on the Arctic Circle.

NADEZDA TALIGINA

(

A PORTFOLIO OF TEN DRAWINGS

The Winter Road (1986)

Shakr: Native Range in Salekhard (1992)

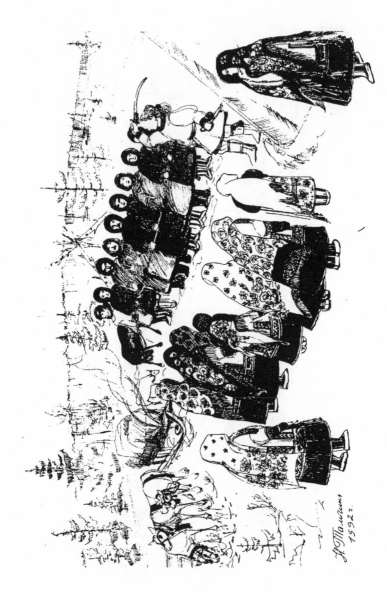

Nae Bory: Wedding Party (1992)

Before the Parting: The Camp (1987)

Porlyty Har: The Sacred Place (1990)

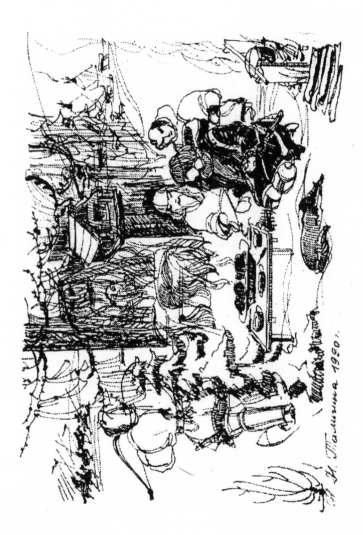

Porlyty Har: The Sacred Place (variation) (1990)

Katra Hot: An Old House (1988)

Un Lor: The Big Lake, Waiting (1988)

Uly Talala: Funeral (1996)

Yush Tuty Khy: Man-Following-the-Road (1992)

Yuri Vaella (TAIGA NENETS)

(

Like Yeremei Aipin, **Yuri Kilevich (Aivaseda) Vaella** was born in the village of Varyogan in West Siberia in 1948. He is of the taiga Nenets people, who historically lived along the Pur River. During the Civil War of 1918-19, however, growing increasingly destitute, the Nenets moved south from the tundra to the Agan River in the taiga forest and adopted the culture of the Khanty reindeer people. Aivaseda takes his pseudonym—*Vaella*—from an ancient taiga Nenets clan.

Vaella's first teacher was his grandmother, who introduced him to the oral tradition. As a teenager, Vaella spent a number of years in a boarding school, then went into the army, working as a carpenter. In the 1980s, again like Aipin, he studied creative writing at the Moscow State Literary University. He began to publish in 1988, writing poetry, short stories, and sketches in both Nenets and Russian. A reindeer owner who spends most of his time in his ancestral deer camp grounds, Vaella is the head of the Association of Private Reindeer Owners. His stand against the oil industry's invasion of his native territorial grounds has always been strident. In 1989 he organized the first picket line among Khanty hunters to protest the encroachment of the oil barons. In his native village of Varyogan he established the Museum of Traditional Culture of the Taiga People.

Vaella has written and published folktales, poems, essays,

and has recorded folksongs. His poetry appears in the leading Russian literary magazines. His volume of collected poems, *White Cries,* was published in Surgut in 1996, followed by three more books of prose and poetry. Some of his works have been trans-lated into English, Hungarian, German, French, Finnish, Estonian, and recently into some Muslim languages of Siberia.

AT THE BUS STOP

Trolley Route 29. Moscow. Early morning.
Final stop, Dynamo Stadium.

I am standing by the booth
at the bus stop
reading scraps of newspaper ads:
"Exchange."
"Urgent exchange . . ."
"Separation."
"Needed: 3-room apartment
with balcony facing South.
In 5 years
a new Metro line
will reach here. . . ."
"5-room apartment,
with a lounge,
in exchange for 2 apartments.
Any kind,
one must be in or near Moscow,
another—any part of Russia."
And suddenly I think:
has it come to that?
One day where the reindeer paths cross
my clansmen
will implore:
"Family split,
exchanging tipis. . . ."
"Alcoholic husband,
swapping families. . . ."
"Quarrel with son-in-law,
changing clans. . . ."

WATCHING TV

Joy and sadness live together.
— Nenets proverb

What joy in camp today!
My uncle has a new dweller
in his tipi—a TV set.
The fire cracks in the stove,
children scramble in front,
and grandpa sits in shadows
cradling his chin.
On a blue screen
one movie follows another,
fears, sobs, and songs,
smiles
of the Big World
pouring into this small one.
And grandpa keeps his silence,
sitting in shadows,
knitting his eyebrows,
cradling his chin.
The parachute over the waterfall
hovers, hovers
like a little cloud,
a bird,
a dandelion,
changing the expression
on the faces of
my aunt,
my children,

my uncle,
my grandma,
and my neighbors
who come to marvel at this new wonder.
Yet my grandpa is not amazed;
he looks gloomy today,
sitting in shadows,
with knitted eyebrows,
cradling his chin. . . .
And in the evening
Grandma tells me a secret:
that yesterday,
on his way to the drilling station,
Grandpa dug out
two carcasses of beheaded reindeer
missing a few months ago
from a nearby camp.

ON THINGS ETERNAL
(from a poetic cycle)

You are your native country
you are your native country's eyes
and mind
and conscience
and heart
and so there's no excuse
if your country
by your idleness turns
into camps decaying from time,
into cold and deserted
orphaned hearths
where even the wind has nothing to latch on to
no place to spend the night,
where the lonely beast
searching for food or carrion
stumbles upon it in hunger.
Only the wind-beaten cradle
will remind you
of the child's cry,
of lullabies sung
by wise gray-haired women,
and the unrealized life
of a lost people.

TO THE BEAR
(from *The Bear Feast*)

"After your paw was shot off,
didn't Nature become one-handed,
didn't Nature become half-handed?"

"Through the muzzle of the rifle
aimed at you,
looking back out of the taiga forest
attentively,
do you think us improved?"

SONG OF THE REINDEER BREEDER

I'd like to be a raindrop
and adorn your eyelashes.
Nga-die!
Nga-die!
I'd like to be a snowflake
and rest on your fur collar,
afraid to touch the warmth of your neck.
Nga-die!
Nga-die!
And when you rush along in a sledge
and the snowy expanses sing to you,
I'd like to be a smile, lighting your face.
Nga-die!
Nga-die!

ETERNAL SKY
(from "Spring Triptych 3")

Somehow, as in my youth, I've begun to look
at the sky again, more and more.
>   —private conversation

What do lovers need?
The sky, one heart to another,
the sky
as seen through happy tears.
Why does a woman smile after childbirth?
Because the sky
lifts the window curtains
like wings,
the sky
fills the whiteness of the nursery
with the song of cranes.
What does a newborn need?
The sky in his eyes
and a voice reaching to the sky.
What do parents dream of?
Their children looking straight
into the sky
instead of staring at their shoes
when talking to friends.
What do we wish a man for his journey?
The sky in front
the sky behind
the sky helping
on the left and right

so he won't lose his step
and fall into the dust.
What does a dying man think of?
The sky
above his neighbor's house,
the eternal sky
across the river.

THE LITTLE SHAMAN AND OTHER STORIES
(from *Ischetka*)

Once upon a time, two old men—one Nenets, one Khanty—
were telling stories as they traveled by boat down a river. The
old Nenets was called Yavunko by the Khanty people because
he was as well known and respected among them as among his
own clansmen. Likewise, the old Khanty was called Capitjaay
by the Nenets. The two old men were great friends and Great
Storytellers, each capable of casting a spell on ordinary listen-
ers and master storytellers alike.

At one point the river turned in a large loop before continuing downstream. If you paddled the length of the loop, you
would lose much time. But at the base of the loop there was a
small portage, about twenty paces, so you could carry your boat
across and go right on your way.

Well, Yavunko and Capitjaay were traveling down the
river and telling stories to each other. When they reached the
portage, they carried their boat across and set out again, paddling and paddling. But without knowing it, they had turned
upriver, into the large loop. So on they went, telling stories. At
noon they returned to the portage, carried their boat across,
and started upriver again, back through the loop. They were so
taken by each other's stories that they camped for the night, a
second night as well, amusing themselves beside the fire by telling stories. All in all, in three days' time, they carried their boat
across that portage seven times. Such was the power of their
art—such is the power of true storytellers—that they simply forgot about everything else.

By the way, two of these stories survive. If you tell one of
them in the evening, it will bring a blizzard by morning, or perhaps sleet, for the entire day. The other story will bring clear,

sunny weather. I myself have used these stories several times in my life to bring the weather I wanted. But that has nothing to do with this story.

To this day that place on the river is known as the Loop of the Seven Turns.

MORNING AT THE LAKE

Two mists happened to meet by the lake. One was from the lake itself—a pink one. The other—a purple one—came from the forest.

"Who are you?" the first one asked.

"I am the mist," the second replied.

"But I'm the mist, too."

"Then why don't I see you?"

"I don't see you either . . ."

And all the while a young deer lay in a nearby thicket, chewing grass, eyes closed, seeing and hearing everything.

FYODOR THE HUNTER

"They say you're making a museum."

"Sort of . . ."

"Bringing houses from the camps into the village?"

"Yes."

"Did you bring the *labaz* of the late Kazamin Fyodor?"

"Not yet . . ."

"Then let me tell you a story, and whatever your response, I'll say: 'It's merely the Apocalypse.'"

(

At the time of the war with Hitler the hunters and fishermen of Siberia became very important. Those who weren't good at hunting and fishing were sent to the front. And those who came home—some armless, some legless—said how hard it was there. Pure Apocalypse! But those who stayed at home said they'd rather have gone to war, that the real Apocalypse was right here. The state demanded furs, fish, and meat, yet you had to provide for your own family and children. But how? From every catch you could keep only the smallest fish—like ruff—for yourself. The rest was shipped to the front.

So the children grew up on ruff. That's why, to this day, I can't think of a better meal than ruff soup.

Well, Kazamin Fyodor was the best hunter in these parts. They say he'd won a medal for his furs. He used to hunt sable up the Agan Uval, in the Van-Egan basin.

He'd go with his family to where the *yagel*-moss ended, and there they'd put up their main *choom*. Farther on they'd set up a smaller *choom* for Fyodor, and his wife would take their deer team back to the *yagel* area. Fyodor would stay alone in the taiga for a long time. And true to the hunter's rule, his first chore was to gather as much firewood as possible, stacking it inside the *choom* on both sides of the entrance, with lots of extra outside.

One day while hunting on skis he fell through the ice. He managed to escape but lost his skis, barely making it back to the *choom* as his legs slowly froze. The following day he fell into a fever. A week later his frozen joints began to rot, then gangrene set in, so he scraped the dead flesh from his feet with a knife. And when he got to the bones, he sawed them off with a handsaw.

He had to parcel out the firewood until his wife returned. And he kept telling himself: "It's a good thing, Fyodor, that you gathered so much wood while you were able." By the time his wife came for him, there were only chips left for kindling.

But he had dried his sawed-off legs and buried them in the *labaz*. And he told his relatives: "When I die, put my legs in my coffin, so I won't be burdened with looking for my limbs in the afterlife."

This takes me back to my childhood: I remember a deer team coming toward the collective farm store, and a legless man—wearing a medal on his Native deerskin coat—slid down from the sledge. He crawled on his knees toward the high front porch of the store, pushing a smaller sledge, which he always had with him for his crutches. Then he climbed onto the porch and disappeared through the painted door, leaving the little sledge unguarded outside. I remember being tempted to take that sledge for a ride down a nearby hill. But I was afraid of the handicapped man with the medal on his coat.

NEWS FROM VATYEGAN CAMP

"Old Man Ustya of the Aivaseda clan had a disaster last winter."

"What happened?"

"He was hunting for squirrels in the Vatyegan forests, right where the oil pipeline cuts through, and as the deer team pulled his sledge across a frozen lake the ice suddenly gave way.

"*Dehai-hov!*"

"He said he wasn't worried. He knew that the lake there is breast deep for deer. So he pointed the leader toward the nearest woods, but all at once the deer were covered in black slime, and then his own boots and coat turned black. The smell set his head spinning—'Pure Apocalypse!' he said. He put his hand to his face—oil!"

"*Pimans-kuchahku!*"

"As it turned out, that wasn't a lake but a storage pit. There'd been an accident—the oil had spilled into the lake. You can't see it because of the snow. Old Man Ustya tried to wash the deer, but they froze and died. He himself went blind from the oil. Now all he does is get drunk on the alcohol the oilmen bring into camp. And sing of his pain."

Galina Keptuke (EVENK)

(

Galina Keptuke, a prose writer of the Evenk people, was born in the village of Kukushka, Amur Oblast, East Siberia, in 1951. She takes her name, which means "animal tracker," from a clan that in ancient times migrated through the Amur region along the Jeltula River. The Evenks, who number twenty-nine thousand people, live in the huge area between the Sea of Okhotsk and the Irtysh River. Keptuke's forefathers were hunters and shamans.

From 1969 to 1974 Keptuke did her undergraduate studies at the Leningrad Hertzen Pedagogical Institute, then went to work as a schoolteacher in Yakutia, regularly visiting the Jeltula River region of her ancestors. In 1984 in Leningrad she was granted her Ph.D. for her work on the Evenk language. Subsequently, she has done much fieldwork, recording old Evenk epics and publishing scholarly works on the Evenk language and folklore. She is deeply interested in the shamanistic practices of her ancestors.

Keptuke writes both in Russian and her native Evenk. She is well known for her autobiographical novella *On the Banks of the Jeltula* (1989). Her prose collection *Little America* was published in Moscow in 1991. She lives in Yakutsk.

A DISCOVERY

(from *On the Banks of the Jeltula*)

How I love you, oh clear and light Jeltula! Once again we meet, but this time I see the rushing streams at your headwaters. Big trout hide in your deep pools, salmon leap through your sparkling shallows, ducks nest in your coastal lakes. And now, on your sandy beaches—the voices of children!

Your shores are good, the ground firm; reindeer hooves sound clearly where you flow. No mist or marsh dulls you, and birch groves stretch for miles along your way.

The summer covering of our lodge is full of holes, so Father will strip much birch bark here; Mother will boil it in water, and we will all make a new dress for our summer dwelling.

The day is cool, the wind blowing. There are no mosquitoes, no gadflies. Now the wind is stronger, the leaves noisier and noisier. The wind comes in waves, stronger and stronger, more and more. Mother muffles the bells on the necks of the reindeer so we won't frighten away any moose that might encounter our caravan.

Suddenly we stop—somewhere other bells are ringing. Strange, for we're alone in these parts. What bells are these? When the wind blows, they are clearer and louder. Father turns our reindeer in the direction of the sound. Now the wind is gone, and gone are the bells. Who or what calls to meet us on our way?

Now the sound is nearer and stronger. Surely, people and reindeer will soon appear through the trees. But where are they? There's no one there, yet the bells are loud and clear. We, the children, grow silent. Our reindeer team moves quietly and warily. The deer listen, snort, and stomp the ground.

Our dogs have run ahead and vanished—no barking, no whines, as when two teams meet. Only the sound of hooves, and the wariness. But the bells are right here! Yet it's not the sound of bells on the necks of deer. They ring from above, and the sound flows over us, touching the tops of the birches. There is something eerie about it. It's frightening and troubles the soul.

Father halts the caravan; we climb down from the deer and stand, holding the harness in our hand. Mounting the lead deer, father heads for the bells. They are right next to us, somewhere. Trunks of birches surround us, but we see no one, nothing. What is this mysterious sound? Is it Balbuka, the treacherous forest man, who is confusing our team into following his steps? Why did father go alone? We should turn back, run away, to escape the heart-breaking sound of those bells!

Suddenly our dog Uptan rushes from the birches, circles our team, and runs off after father. I think the bells carry bad news. "Something is going to happen," I think. And it's not my thought alone—all of us are thinking the same thing.

The time passes too slowly. When will Father return? Then, just as my heart is overwhelmed with fear, our lead deer appears through the trees, and my fear recedes. Father is back.

He speaks quietly to Mother, we mount the deer once more, and descend to the riverbank as the bells ring and ring. . . .

Hurriedly we arrange a temporary camp, remove the packs from the reindeer, and light several smoky fires against the mosquitoes. The weary deer lie down to rest. We have to water them and bring green twigs for them to eat. We don't unharness them. Then we drink tea. Father takes out his lariat and ax, his hunting knife always at his side. He calls my brother Sile and they go toward the bells. Mother does not explain anything to the rest of us. If there is anything to know, they will tell us.

Some time later, my father and brother come back down the bank. Father carries two old bells in his hand, on a thick rusty wire. Sile carries the lariat and ax. We are not allowed to touch the bells or ring them. Sile says that the bells were hanging on a tree, left by someone long ago, because the wire cut deeply into the birch trunk. They had been put on a young birch that is now big, the wire in so deep that they had to cut it. The wire was thoroughly rusted and fragile. The bells were on a branch, not the main trunk. How much longer would they have hung there? Not for long, it seems. The strong wind would have snapped the rusty wire, and the bells would have fallen to the ground. Maybe that's why they had been ringing so urgently—the time had come for someone to find them. And it happened to be my father.

What does this discovery mean? Who put those bells on that tree, and why? I don't know yet. Mother gets out the *inmack*, the beautifully embroidered sack for special family possessions, and puts the bells in. Then we pack up and continue on our way.

Toward evening we stop on the banks of the Jeltula. Mother finds some fragrant *ledum* branches to freshen the contents of the *inmack*. Then she purifies with smoke our sacred deer Durbai, its beautiful harness, and our *kumulan* carpet. Evening descends, the sun sets, and the deer graze freely. We tie up the dogs and put a hood on the noisy puppy. One thing is certain— tonight, Father will sing the *dyarichin*, the prayer-song. He does this from time to time, and we children must help him. He will ask the spirit of the Jeltula for good hunting and good luck. Or perhaps something else.

In summer we prepare our meals outside, over a fire. But today the fire is kindled in a stove, for ceremonial purposes, although it is summer and the evenings are hot. Our lodge warms quickly. Then mother raises the rear wall and brings in the *inmack*.

We begin to drink tea. The firewood has burned down to red coals in the stove. Father begins to sing, and we repeat every line after him. We are alone out here. Except for our parents, there are no Evenks around; so we children must help

Father with his singing. Because the *dyarichin* is a prayerful request expressed in song, it is asked on behalf of all Evenks, ourselves included. The singer is followed by the choir. Ours consists of my mother, my brother, my sisters, and me. Only Ayakchan, the youngest, is excused because she is too little and confuses the words.

My father's voice is strong and pleasant:

> O mother Jeltula,
> your children have come to you,
> we have come to your banks
> and made our camp here.

And our chorus follows:

> Mother Jeltula,
> you feed your children, the Evenks,
> and we are grateful!
> Be a friend to us always,
> and give us rich game;
> do not let our hearth die out;
> let our children grow up!
> We sing this request
> on behalf of everyone.

We follow along as Father sings, while Mother puts pieces of fat on the stove, then the fragrant *ledum* branches. The aromas mix pleasantly and delight our noses. Father smokes, rests a while, then resumes his singing:

> O Mother Jeltula!
> What a strange gift you have given today!
> Tell me: is it for good or evil?

Mother offers Father a silver spoon from the *inmack,* one not used for eating. Repeating the question, Father throws the spoon. We watch apprehensively. How will it land? Which side up? But it falls the right way, as if placed on a table. We sigh with relief, but Mother gives us a look of reproach—we must not betray our feelings. She returns the spoon to Father, saying "*Tavachae.*" It has fallen the right way! Father takes the spoon, sings once more, and we repeat, echoing his words of gratitude for the strange gift of the Jeltula. The meaning is clear: there is no bad news in the bells from the birch tree! Something good will come soon! Thank you, oh Native river, for the gift, and for wishing us well!

"My river wouldn't have wished me ill," I reason, "for my cry was first heard on her banks. I was born on the Jeltula."

We drink more tea and go to bed, knowing all will be well.

(

For many days we camp in that place. Father gathers much birch bark, Mother boils it with herbs, and we make a new covering for our summer dwelling. We line the long strips of birch bark with cloth to cover our *dukcha.* We make a new *inmack* as well and keep the bells in it. One of these bells will be given to me, I think, for my she-deer has recently lost hers. But one is put on Durbai's neck and the other remains in the new *inmack.*

During all of this time I try to learn from my Mother the meaning of our find. I listen to her conversations with Father, hoping to hear something new. When they mention the shaman Sodorchan, the one who cured my grandfather, I listen carefully to my Father's words:

There's not a single shaman left in our clan now, and this is bad. Sodorchan would have lived longer had his relatives done what he had told them to do. Now even *their* clan is dying out. So who is left? Only Nekchor and his family. Yes, the people have stopped following the old customs; they have begun to die out. All of that happened because of Sodorchan's relatives.

Sodorchan once told his younger brother: "You will kill a moose soon. You will kill it on the banks of the Jeltula, where Ollongro Creek enters. Then you will kill an elk in the same place. Bring him to me, the head and the hide, and I shall make medicine." But Nekchor didn't do it. He took the elk's meat to the mining camp and sold it there. Later, Sodorchan said again: "You will kill another moose soon. When you begin to pack the meat, an elk will come to you, trumpeting. Kill him, and bring me the meat." But again his brother sold the meat at the mining camp and did not bring the head to Sodorchan.

That elk, father continues, was intended for making big medicine. Sodorchan was going to ask the goddess Ayihit to restore the good old life of his clan. But the ritual was never performed, and his clan began to die out. I helped him make medicine many times. Sodorchan loved me very much.

Once, when I was on my way to Bomnak, carrying goods for an expedition, the prosecutor overtook me and asked:

"Do you know Sodorchan, the shaman? They say he's still making medicine. They'll have to take him into custody."

"Why should he be put in custody?" I said. "He does no harm. On the contrary, he cured my father some time ago. He's no killer, no evil doer."

"Don't you realize that the Soviet Power is against shamans?"

"Yes, I do, but Sodorchan is a good man; there's no need for him to go to prison!"

"You sound just like him. Are you defending shamanism? Are you ready for custody yourself? If you want to stay out of prison, you must put it in writing to me that the shaman Sodorchan is evil because he continues his rituals. You must testify that he is against the Soviet Power."

"But he does nothing against the Soviet Power, and he

hasn't harmed anyone!" And then I told him, "You are literate, but you're a fool just the same. If you're a prosecutor, you
must *prove* him guilty before you take him to prison. And I'm
not going to prison either. You could have helped me, that time
they charged me for nothing—everybody knows I didn't eat the
prison camp's deer. Until fools like you go to prison, I won't
be put there! Did they teach you how to write just to put good
people in jail?"

That's exactly what I told him, and I didn't go on to Bomnak. Later, when I met Sodorchan, he said they had found
someone to write against him. "Your signature wasn't there,"
he said. "Thank you for not wanting to harm me." Then he
made medicine and foretold a good life for me. "Your children
will become good people," he said.

I did not see Sodorchan after that. He was taken away and
must have died in prison somewhere. A good man gone for
nothing. Oh, Sodorchan was a powerful shaman, all right! He
could make you blind, or he could make you do what he wanted.
When he began to make medicine and sing, everyone saw and
did what he saw and did. When some shamans make medicine,
they go traveling, yet they cannot take people along with them.
But Sodorchan would take them to the uppermost sky, and to
the underworld as well. But he never used his power for evil. . . .

Here a mosquito bites me, I scratch the spot, and my father's tale stops. But I beg him: "Daddy, tell me, please tell me,
about Sodorchan's drum and regalia! How they returned to him
three times! Sile told me once, but I forgot!"

My father smiles. It's a sad story, he says, yet a funny one.
Funny because that prosecutor, whose name was Romanov, had
really had it with the old man before they took him to prison.
But it's a happy story as well, because even the Russians came
to believe in Sodorchan's power. The police themselves didn't
want to take Sodorchan away, but the prosecutor got him arrested all the same. And this Romanov was an Evenk! As a boy,

he was saved by Sodorchan from sinking in a bog, and Sodorchan restored the boy's sanity.

"Daddy!" I cry out. "I remember! Isn't this prosecutor the boy who was scared out of his wits?"

"That's him. People don't remember the good that's done to them."

Father pauses, then continues:

When Sodorchan was taken for the first time by the police, under someone else's accusation, he was brought to the prosecutor. When the old man saw an Evenk like himself, he was pleased. When he recognized the boy in Romanov, he wanted to talk to him in Evenk, but the prosecutor sat as silent and impenetrable as a rock.

"Speak Russian, please," he said.

Sodorchan's eyes almost popped out in amazement. "You know I speak Russian badly. It will be easier to explain things in Evenk."

"Don't forget where you are!" the prosecutor shouted. "You're not in the taiga, you're not among your deer! You're in a Soviet institution!"

Well, the old man sort of sunk down, shocked. They began to interrogate him. Sodorchan tried to explain everything, but in vain. The prosecutor had forgotten his old ways.

"Sonny," Sodorchan said. "You're an Evenk, aren't you? You must know that a shaman can't stop making medicine—he must do his job. That's how he is. I'm not against the Soviet Power. You can't do away with such a power by making medicine. The Soviet Power does many good things for us Evenks."

"Tell me this, then," the prosecutor replied. "Why were you visited by the mother of a youngster we wanted to educate in Leningrad? Didn't she ask you to make medicine so he wouldn't be sent away?"

"Oh no, Sonny," Sodorchan answered. "She asked me to make medicine for the road, so he'd have a good journey. His road was to be different, and long—not a road that every Evenk takes. And so I made sure that nothing bad would happen to him in distant lands."

All his life Sodorchan told me that he had never lied to anyone, except then. But those who had written against him were telling lies as well.

Romanov was offended. So Sodorchan looked at him and said, "Don't you remember when I helped you with your troubles? I made medicine then, too. I didn't want to remind you—it's not our custom to accept payment for what we do. You couldn't have forgotten! You were seven then, old enough to remember."

Well, at this point the prosecutor turned livid and began to shout and stomp his feet. "It never happened! Don't try to pin an anti-Soviet action on me! I can make powder out of people like you!"

That's exactly what he said: *I can make powder out of you!* And he calls himself literate. Everybody knows you can't turn a person into powder. Well, he shouted at length and made threats. And not a word of Evenk came out of him—he had forsaken his mother tongue. He wouldn't help the one who had saved him. Finally, he called for a policeman and sent him away with Sodorchan to fetch his drum and shaman's regalia.

When they got to his tent, Sodorchan said to the policeman, "Have some tea, Sonny." This policeman was so young—a Russian—and he didn't refuse. So they had tea, then Sodorchan packed his things in a sack and handed it over. The policeman returned to the village, locked the sack in a cabinet, and went home. When he got to work in the morning, the prosecutor sent for him.

"Now show me his drum," he demanded.

The policeman took the sack from the cabinet, but there was nothing inside. Romanov scolded him: "You're a shaman's helper! You want to cheat me! You pitied the Dark One!"

The poor guard didn't know what to say, for with his own eyes he had seen the old man put his things into that sack and hand it over. So they returned to Sodorchan's tent and the prosecutor ordered a search. The old man didn't resist. He was cooperative. Once again he packed everything in a sack and gave it to them. Then the policeman took Sodorchan aside for a moment so the prosecutor couldn't hear.

"Tell me, Father," he asked. "How did your things disappear from the sack? You put them in before my very eyes. You couldn't have stolen them from the cabinet!"

"I didn't steal anything," Sodorchan answered. "You'll understand later."

So they returned to the village, Romanov stopping twice on the way to check the sack, and when they arrived it was again locked away in the cabinet. The following day Romanov sent a young boy to Zeya to deliver the sack there in order to show his superiors that one more shaman had been rendered harmless. But a week later he received a telegram: "What kind of joke is this?" it read. "Why did you send us a sack of muck? Where is the drum?"

Well, the prosecutor went mad and ordered a search for Sodorchan, who had gone to the taiga. But there's no real way to hide there, so they found him and brought him back to the village. Again there were interrogations, and again Romonov took everything from Sodorchan and locked it in the cabinet. Sodorchan himself was put into custody for resisting the Soviet Power. But he hadn't resisted; he had given his things willingly, so there was no way to detain him.

Again Romanov sent the sack to Zeya, and again the same thing happened. No drum in the sack! So Sodorchan went to trial and was condemned for stealing his own things from the cabinet! The young policeman later said that when he took the old shaman away to prison, Sodorchan said to him:

"I didn't steal my own things. They were always with me. It's just that I covered your eyes."

Suddenly my mother's voice breaks in:

"You shouldn't have quarreled with Romanov. You should have kept silent. Now you can't go to Bomnak."

"Should we keep silent when a man is accused for nothing," my father says, "and commit an injustice?"

Mother doesn't respond.

"What will you do now?" she asks finally. "Accept your fate? There are no shamans left, I'm afraid. The Soviet Power doesn't approve of them. If someone from the prison finds out that you are destined to be a shaman, it won't be good for us. We have children. They may be persecuted, too."

And so the meaning of those bells is finally clear to me. They are a sign that my father must become a shaman—a long and difficult road.

THE UNEXPECTED GUEST
(from *On the Banks of the Jeltula*)

All summer we have been migrating along the right bank of the Jeltula River. Now we must cross to the other side. But in order to do so, we have to get to the very headwaters, to cross the divide by the grave of Granddaddy Paskene.

I never saw Granddaddy Paskene alive. I only know of him through the stories of my father, mother, Old Man Charikte, and Sile. He died when Sile was just three or four, but Sile told me he remembers him well. He remembers his tales, the *nimnakans*. Granddaddy Paskene could tell stories all night long—he knew so many. Among the Evenk, *nimnakans* are not only told but sung. But it's difficult now to find an Evenk who can sing them. Yes, Charikte sings a little, but he says he's nothing compared to Granddaddy Paskene. Whenever they talk about Granddaddy Paskene, I feel like he wasn't so much a man who passed away as a fire that's gone out. *Paskene* means *spark*. There was a spark, a fire, but now that fire is gone. Its bright sparks are no more. Gone is the spark of Granddaddy Paskene.

When we talk about him, my mother muses: who will take up his gift? His skill of relating the *nimnakans* must be passed on. If a fire is gone, you can kindle a new one. People know how to kindle a fire and care for it. Sooner or later, my mother says, Granddaddy Paskene will send a spark, and the spark will begin to burn in the heart of another man. It won't let him alone until he becomes a storyteller. But to become a *nimnakanlan* is as difficult as becoming a shaman. The storyteller, like the shaman, must endure many ordeals. That's what everyone says.

Granddaddy Paskene's grave is on our way, but it's not a custom among the Evenk to visit graves. In fact, they're avoided. But Granddaddy Paskene's grave is located in such a way that it's impossible to avoid. He is buried at the foot of the divide through which we must pass, and there is no other road to take. Right here on our route Granddaddy Paskene's *soul-heyan* left him. Here he lies buried. And my mother says it isn't by chance. From those who pass by, he will choose one to whom to send his spark. "Have no fear of me when you pass by," they say he said before his death. "Give me some tobacco, and I shall send you some game. If you'd like to know how long you will live, lie on your back over my grave. If you dare do so, you'll know what I wish for you." But to date no one has dared, for it's better to live without knowing what lies ahead. My father always treats Paskene to tobacco, and the old man never lets him down—a mile or so ahead my father always kills a moose.

Soon the grave will appear. We are getting closer. Then we stop our caravan while Mother lights a paper cigarette and leaves it on the grave. When she mounts her deer again, we continue. But my father and Sile linger at the grave. Mother calls Sile, but he doesn't seem to hear. He just stays with Father. So we go on without looking back—it is forbidden to look back at a grave. Then, having ridden for some distance, we make camp. When my father and Sile return, my father is obviously in good spirits. After tea, at playtime, I listen to what he tells my mother:

"Our son is brave. I never thought he'd dare test his fate."

"And you allowed him to do so?"

"Whoever dares such a thing is no coward. He has a strong heart. A strong heart will chase away fear. Trouble clings only to fear. But Sile had no fear, so I allowed him."

I run to find Sile and learn the details. Yes, my brother tried to learn his destiny. He lay on Granddaddy Paskene's grave for a long time. He said he wasn't afraid because he re-members Granddaddy Paskene well, and he's not the least bit afraid of him now that he's dead. He even felt some warmth coming from the earthen mound. My father said this is good. If cold came from the grave, it would be a bad omen. "Paskene

wished you a good life," my father explained. And so it must
be. . . .

Crossing a river is a serious matter. You must obey all the
customs. At the last campsite Mother prepared a new long rope
out of tanned buckskin. And she gave each of us multicolored
strips of cloth for gifts. My own gift to Jeltula is a teaspoon. My
sister Tambe wants to offer her cup with the blue flowers on it.
But before we reach the river we must cross one last mountain.
When we reach the summit, we continue on and approach the
descent. From the top of the mountain you can see the river cutting around the ridges, rushing into the open ground below. As
we descend, the Jeltula is often lost behind the trees, then suddenly it flashes in the taiga clearings—like the knife of a hunter
working his kill in the sun.

Our caravan halts at the river. My mother fastens the rope to
two birches on the riverbank, and along that rope we fasten our
many-colored strips. I leave my new spoon here, and my sister
puts her cup near a birch tree. While we do this, my father steps
to the edge of the river and makes a plea. He speaks quietly and
we repeat after him, addressing the river with the same words:

> O great river of sacred power!
> O big river that we call Jeltula!
> Let us safely cross over!
> Take us to your far shore!

Mother breaks some small willow branches and binds them
into three bundles of six branches each. We sit on the deer and
Father starts across with Old Man Charikte. Mother follows
with Sile and me, then the other children—Tambe, Morso, and
Ayakchan. As soon as the deer team enters the river, my mother
drops the first bundle from her right hand into the water. She
addresses the river:

O big river that we call Jeltula!
O great river of sacred power!
I am a mother—I, too, have children!
Let us safely cross over!

As we reach the middle of the river, she throws another bundle
into the water. And as the last deer emerges on the far bank, the
river is given a third bundle. Then we dismount, and my mother
thanks the river, saying:

O sacred and powerful river that we call Jeltula!
You have let us cross well!
Please do so in the future, for me and my children!

On this bank, too, we offer the nearest bushes bright strips of
cloth, and as our caravan ascends the high bank, I look back.
The wind is playing with the cloth strips. They are waving at us
in a friendly manner, wishing us a good journey.

In the valley of the Jeltula River there are many lakes where
ducks and geese nest. It's the end of August now and the fledg-
lings have grown up. Soon they will fly south for the first time
and see new lands. But they will return nevertheless to their
native nests. The Evenks are like that. Like migrating birds, we
see many lands when on the move but never leave our native
land for good. Evenks always return home. If ever I leave you,
oh Jeltula, I will return just the same. I will come back and request a happy crossing, once again putting bright strips of cloth
on your riverbank, brought from far-off lands.

The weather starts to worsen and we stop to make camp.
The wind strengthens and clouds rush in, filling the sky. It begins to rain. A drizzle at first and then a downpour. The deer
wander off, grazing, while the dogs hide under the tarpaulin
thrown over the bushes for shelter. As it gets wet, the green

tarpaulin of our tent grows lighter in color, turning yellow as the day moves toward sunset.

The fire in the stove warms the tent and it is hot inside. Even on the outside the chimney is red from the heat. When raindrops strike it, it hisses angrily and makes steam. Soon the rain grows stronger, overwhelming the chimney, and there's no more steam. But it's still hot, so I open the flap and secure it. You can see the river far off. Not the river itself, but a thick strip of mist. Toward evening the mist falls to the river and a smoky layer covers all. But suddenly in the mist a dark spot appears. It moves quickly right toward us. It's a goose! And I think: where are you going, stupid! Why did you leave your dry hummock or warm nest?

"A goose!" I cry, pointing my finger. "It's flying this way!"

But there's no time for anyone to grasp my words before the goose noisily lands—right on our warm chimney! I sit by the tent flap, unafraid, and study it carefully. When I look behind me, my mother sits frozen, her cup of tea halfway to her mouth. My father is on his knees, gazing at the tarpaulin wall by the chimney. Old Man Charikte holds an unlit match in his hand, having forgotten about it. In his other hand is a matchbox. His pipe is about to fall from his mouth. Sile and the others sit full of fear, mouths wide open. All are afraid. Why? I alone have no fear. A word drops from my lips, and the goose, hearing an unusual sound, lifts off, heavily flapping its wings, disappearing into the mist and rain. Everyone remains motionless for some time, but I run to the back of the tent, afraid now, too.

"Your future spirit-helper has come," Old Man Charikte concludes.

Father is silent.

I have heard that when a man is to become a shaman, his future spirit-helpers visit him. It may be a goose, duck, swan, crane, cuckoo bird, or many others. They will help him fly to the Upper World. There are also helpers among the beasts and fish.

If a man refuses, his spirit-helpers will try to make a shaman out of him nonetheless. They will send him an illness called "turning in circles." And he will roam the taiga, in circles, losing his mind. What's my father to do? Should he become a shaman? As it is today, to become a shaman is bad; yet not to become one is even worse. If the spirits are angry, they may take away my father's mind for good.

Who will show my father the ways of the shaman?

(

Something is happening to Father. Yesterday evening, after the goose flew away, he started to sing the *dyarichin*. But this time his song was different. We all helped him, but I understood next to nothing—first he trumpeted like a crane, then he chirped like a tomtit. He was arguing with someone and didn't want to give in. The night's songs were unclear to me. My father didn't sleep. Then he spent the morning preparing to go upriver. By noon Old Man Charikte became worried and went after him. My mother was ill at ease; nothing went right for her. We waited for my father and Charikte, but they remained away. The day drew to a close, and they didn't return.

Where did my father go? Why didn't he say anything to Mother? Why didn't he take his gun with him? No, he wasn't hunting. If he were, Mother wouldn't worry and Charikte wouldn't go after him. What's happening to my father? More and more he turns inward, now and again responding strangely, as if his thoughts are occupied by something we don't know. Often he begins speaking to someone invisible, reasoning with him, answering back. Several times I heard him say—either to himself or his invisible adversary—"I don't know where they are, those paths. Show them to me!" My father wants to go somewhere but doesn't know the way. Yet he knows every path in our taiga forest. Even if he has never been to a place, he can find it. So what are these paths that my father can't find? Such thoughts torment me all day. Have the future spirit-helpers beset him already, sending him in mad circles?

Losing patience, I find a good moment to approach my mother:

"What are these paths that Father is looking for?"

"Hush!" she reponds. "You're always sticking your nose everywhere! Haven't you seen the red moose that your father killed? And still you ask, what is he looking for! He's received a sign to become a shaman. Yet how is that done nowadays? To be a shaman, you have to know the shaman's ways. These must be shown to the novice by an old and experienced shaman. And where would you find one now?"

"But Charikte can make medicine!"

"Charikte is the shaman of the Sologon clan. He has his own paths to follow. Don't you know your own father's clan? Each shaman must follow the paths of his clan. Charikte has his ways, and your father must have his own."

"But who will show him the way?"

"There's no one. That's the problem. Great difficulties lie ahead for your father, and I don't know what will come of it."

"What if he can't find the path?"

"I don't know, I don't know what will happen." My mother falls silent.

Later, playing with Sile on the riverbank, I ask: "Will Father fall ill?" But without waiting for an answer, I continue: "To become a shaman is to lose your mind."

"That's what I think, too," Sile answers.

Somewhere nearby a cuckoo bird begins to sing. Rather, it squawks like a chicken, for in August the cuckoos stop singing. It's said that the very first cuckoo, created by the god Seveki, found a host of ripe blueberries and ate so many that its throat swelled and it could no longer sing. That's why cuckoos stop singing when the blueberries ripen. And since the blueberries stay ripe for so long, the cuckoo can only squawk from time to time, just like a chicken. Their squawking means it will rain.

Thinking about this, I suddenly remember something my mother told me that she learned from Granddaddy Paskene. If you kill a cuckoo bird and spend the night under the tree where it perched, you will see a vision after you roast it on an iron spit. When you eat the roasted cuckoo, you make a wish, and your wish will be answered in a dream. I remind Sile about it, and his eyes brighten with a gleam I cannot understand.

"Wait here. I'll be back in a minute," he says, then runs to the tent.

I continue playing and soon he comes back with a rifle. It's his own gun and he can use it as he likes.

"What are you going to do? You mustn't kill cuckoos!"

"Yes you can, if there's a medicine man to forgive your sin. We'll tell Charikte later and he'll do it for us. I want to know what my father has to do."

And without waiting for my approval, Sile crawls toward the tree where the cuckoo bird perches. I stay where I am. I cannot walk the taiga soundlessly, so I don't make a move. "Sile's right," I think to myself, "we can do something so our father doesn't suffer. But how will Sile arrange to spend the night under the tree? We can't let anyone know, or Mother won't let him do it. We must think of something!"

A gunshot interrupts my thoughts.

"Come here!" Sile calls. He is standing beneath the tree with a cuckoo bird in his hands.

We quickly make a plan. We will pretend we are playing a game; that we will put up a new tent for ourselves. Then, when everyone falls asleep, Sile will go to the new tent under the tree. Now all we have to do is keep the other children away—Tambe, Morso, and Ayakchan. They might want to sleep there themselves. Well, Ayakchan is easy to get rid of—she likes to sleep with her mother—but Tambe and Morso will insist on sleeping with us. But we'll think of something. We can pick a quarrel, if we have to, and kick them out. Meanwhile, we gather wood and make a huge pile of dry branches, then hang the cuckoo bird from the tree and go away.

Sile scavenges material for a new tent from Mother. She gives permission instantly, to keep us out of her hair, worried by the absence of Father and Charikte. She wants to divert our attention from Father as well. She is even happy when we start to play in the new tent. But Morso and Tambe arrive in a flash. They bring their beds with them and begin to settle in for the night. Soon it grows dark, and although it is early yet, Sile wants to go to sleep. He spreads out his bed and begins to tell such scary stories that our hair stands on end. He gets so carried away telling about the *chuluro* beasts that the children begin to cry. Then he teases them until they run for their mother. Now it's pitch dark, and although my mother's tent is nearby, it's going to be frightening to sleep alone.

"Shall I pluck the cuckoo's feathers?" I ask Sile.

"What for? I'll fill a kettle with water and bring clay from the bank. Then I'll cover the bird with clay, fix it on a rod, and put it straight into the coals. Later, the feathers will come right off with the clay."

"I'd like to stay with you, if I may."

"No. I must spend the night alone."

The candle flame dances with our movements. Slowly, as if pondering, it bends to one side, then quickly turns to another. We watch and wait until the others are asleep. Finally, the candles in the other tents go out, and we put ours out, too. Sile calls for the dog, and I return quietly to my mother's tent.

My night is long and restless. Sile returns in the morning before my mother is up. And instead of asking what he saw in the dream, I suddenly say, "Was the cuckoo bird tasty?"

I wasn't myself that morning. All night my heart had seemed

stuck to my back, or it was as if it had moved into my stomach. So only one idea was on my mind: "Was the cuckoo bird tasty?"

"Yes, it was," Sile replies, sitting down on my bed. "And you know, I did have a dream. Grandfather Paskene came and said, 'Let your father sing *nimnakans* without stopping, for seven days in a row. One long *nimnakan* for each night. If he can do it, he'll become a *nimnakalan,* and then there's no need for him to become a shaman.'"

I have never heard my father sing the *nimnakans.* He tells short tales rather often. But to sing *nimnakans* all night long—could he do it?

No one knows yet about the cuckoo bird and its secret. We are all doing our chores and waiting for Father and Charikte. Again today my mother doesn't feel well. Her heart aches. But then, after we sit down for tea countless times, Charikte appears. His look bodes ill: he is tired, sweat covers his wrinkled face, and there is a restlessness about him. Usually, Charikte is a joker and a merry storyteller. No matter how tired he might be, he's such fun when he talks about himself that we laugh and laugh. But now he's not in a joking mood. Yet he tries to be.

"Barely made it," he says. "And if I hadn't hurried my dragging feet with a merry song, I wouldn't even be here. First, I sang to my right foot: 'Oh ramrod foot, go ahead, go ahead!' Then I sang to my left foot, even nicer: 'Oh arrow foot, fly quick, fly quick!' And here I am!" He addresses me: "You must memorize my song. When you're old, you can sing it to your feet!"

I smile, for I understand. "You won't trick me, Charikte!" I pretend to laugh.

While Charikte eats quickly, we children are asked to go and play. Even our fat-cheeked Tambe seems to understand. Her thoughts are usually about town, the wonderful toys in the stores there. She always says that when she grows up she will move to town and become a shopkeeper herself. And she won't wear warm fur boots but the white *valenki.* And she'll buy chocolate often. She pronounces the word one syllable at a time, as if to remind us of something. Here's what it was:

Once, when my father had sold his pelts, he brought each of us a big chocolate bar. Instantly Sile, Morso, Ayakchan, and I ate our own, then licked the bright wrappers and tossed them away. But Tambe just stood there, admiring her chocolate bar. Then she hid it in her pocket.

"Eat your chocolate, or I'll take it from you," Sile said, realizing how stupid we were to have devoured ours so greedily.

"No!" Tambe said, getting angry. "You'll get too fat!" She began to nibble her chocolate bar anyway. But after one bite she rewrapped it and said, "Whoever can spell *chocolate* correctly will get half of my candy bar."

I responded the quickest. "C-h-a-c-a-l-a-t-e!"

"No-o-o," Tambe smiled smartly.

"C-h-i-c-k-o-l-a-t-e," Sile said.

"This is what you get," and Tambe made a derisive gesture.

"C-h-i-c-k-o-l-a-t-e," said Morso.

"C-h-e-c-k-o-l-a-d-e!"

"C-h-e-c-k-o-l-a-d-e!"

"C-h-a-c-k-o-l-a-d-e!" we guessed together.

"Well," Tambe said. "I'll have to eat it myself. It's c-h-o-c-o-l-a-t-e!"

We grabbed the wrapper from her hands and devoured the letters with our eyes. Yes, that's the way this sweet word is spelled. And Tambe ate her chocolate by herself. But there was something wrong here. Tambe knew none of us had looked at our wrapper. No one even thought to check. Tambe had made the rules because she was sure she wouldn't have to share her chocolate with any of us. That's how she is.

Sile crawls to the rear wall of the tent, listening to the talk between my mother and Charikte. He can't wait for them to tell the news themselves. Sile breaks many taboos and gets away with it. Even when they shame him, he explains everything in such a way that you have to believe him, as if there were no other way. Yes, my brother knows how to pull your leg. His stories leave you not a foot to hold on to.

Mother calls for Sile and tells him that she will go after my father with Charikte. He's ill and can't come back on his own. And she has a message for me: "Don't be afraid of anything, Gunilgen. We'll be back soon. Father is ill, very ill. Trouble has come to our door, to our hearth. If Father doesn't recover, I don't know how we'll live. You love your father very much, so in whatever state you see him, don't be afraid. He must recognize you. He must."

I want to ask why my father wouldn't recognize me, but suddenly I know: they have stolen his mind!

"Mother!" I cry. "Father won't give in to the circling madness. He's strong! He's sturdy! I don't want it!" I burst into tears, and everyone runs out at my crying and wailing.

Charikte grabs me and embraces me, calming me down. "Child, why are you burying your father before his time? Your tears are a great sin, for he's alive. Wipe your tears. See, you've frightened everyone."

Ayakchan, Morso, and Tambe begin to cry, too. Then my mother snatches the nearest branch, her eyes sparkling with anger.

"So you've buried your father, already?" she says coldly. "Well, who's crying now? Look at me!"

We wipe away our tears and stare at our mother.

"Now all of you, listen to me! When we return, the food must be ready and all the dishes must be clean. Sile, Morso— you go to the rocks and gather a sackful of *kavav*. Let Tambe milk the she-deer and tie up the calves. And you"—she turns to me—"you look after your sister."

Oh, how sorry I was to have burst into tears! One mustn't cry when there's still hope. It's a great sin to cry, causing unnecessary grief. And so I place a spell on myself, just the way my mother does when she's in trouble:

"Harden, oh my heart! Be strong like the birch root! Don't shed sap-tears like young birches in spring! Oh my eyes, don't shed tears! Tears wither the body and soul, and all strength goes with them! You must be strong to survive!"

I must be strong not only in limb, but with something else, something I can't yet express in words. But I already feel it inside me. The very thing that helps my father survive, and my mother, and Charikte. Perhaps my lips will find this word and utter it soon.

All day long Sile and Morso crawl on the rocks along the banks of the Jeltula. The *kavav* herb grows on the rocks, right out of the small cracks where soil and pine needles collect, spreading its stems like the feathers of a hazel grouse. It's dry to the touch, and even feels rough, but its subtle aroma harbors a power within. This herb wards off all sorts of illness. It is sacred, burned by shamans during their rituals, and it is burned over the sacred deer. It wards off not only illness but evil spirits as well. They are frightened of its scent, just like mosquitoes are afraid of smoke. My mother dries this herb and keeps it in a special pouch. But we need a lot of it now, as Mother said. So having done what my mother requested, there's nothing to do but wait.

And so we wait. And wait longer, the entire day. Then the sun begins to drop behind the mountain, and yet my mother and Charikte do not return. I call Sile and ask him: "When will we tell our secret?" My brother thinks about it and says:

"Until our father gets well, he'll be unable to sing a *nimnakan*. When a man is possessed by the circling illness, he remembers nothing. Besides, I lied to you. You can't kill a cuckoo bird without a shaman's permission. I committed a sin to learn what Father must do. If he doesn't get well, evil will befall all of us. So let it come to me only, and maybe I'll learn how to save our father."

The sun is behind the mountain now, and bright colors streak the horizon. Normally, this is when we would choose our colors from the sunset, each of us shouting: "Okay! That blue one beyond—it's mine! That's for my new dress!"

"And the red? The red one is mine!"

The sunset has many colors. It can be bright and unusual, with all the colors of the rainbow. But today it's an ominous dark red. Not merry but frightening, as if someone has smeared the horizon with fresh blood—first one stroke, then another—and then, feeling displeased, painted the entire sky in bloody tones.

It's growing dark, and still we wait. Finally, our dog Uptan runs up. His stomach has shrunk—he must have been without food for a long time. Then mother and Charikte appear. The old man is on foot, leading the deer Vaska by the bridle. Something hangs across the saddle on both sides. Mother follows on her own deer. As they approach, it's clear that my father is draped across the saddle. Mother encourages her deer forward while Charikte falls behind. Then we huddle in the new tent that Sile and I made.

"You sit here awhile," Mother says. "We'll bring your father in ourselves. Come when I call you."

But I bolt from the tent and approach my father. I always run to meet him and do so now. Mother doesn't try to stop me. My father is tied up with ropes, arms and feet, his head wrapped in mother's scarf. His whole face is scratched, bitten by mosquitoes, swollen from gnats' stings. He is either asleep or totally unconscious. I shake him and say:

"It's me, Gunilgen. Open your eyes. Don't you recognize me?"

My father opens his eyes and looks at me, but without recognition. His eyes see nothing. They wander about, then stop, focusing on one point—but where? I don't know.

"This isn't the way, child," Charikte says. "Let him be. He can't recognize you now. It was a long trip. See how we had to carry him? You can't keep a man upside down for very long."

Father is taken down from the deer and carried into the tent. He begins to stir, his eyes full of fear, looking at us again. He tries to break free from the ropes, tries to get on his feet, but Charikte, Mother, and Sile press him to the ground. He rushes and moans, moans so painfully that no one can bear to hear it.

"Whiskey!" my mother cries. "Bring some whiskey!"

Morso rushes to our baggage and brings a bottle. Mother pours a spoonful and begins to feed it to Father. He tries to break loose and the spoon falls down. Whiskey splatters everywhere. Finally, Mother succeeds in pouring about a glassful into him.

"Now begin burning the *kavav*." She motions to us.

We quickly bring in a bowlful of the herb, and the fragrant smoke fills the tent. Father begins to sing. His voice inspires awe—it quavers and rushes from his throat. Then he cries like a crane. It is the cry of a dying crane, breaking my heart, rising high into the night sky and dying there. My father makes gurgling sounds. Foam appears on his lips. Smoke fills the tent and it becomes difficult to breathe. We open the flaps and fresh air rushes in. Father gulps it with his mouth, and his entire body shakes and shakes. His head shakes, too, and he cries and cries like a crane. Then his song grows quieter and quieter, the cry of a crane flying farther and farther away. Then it stops altogether. Father sinks down and no longer tries to break loose. Mother lowers the tent flaps, and the *kavav* smoke envelops Father again.

"Take the bowl out," she says. "He'll be quiet now. The *kavav* smoke brings sleep. He needs to rest."

All night long we keep Father inside the smoky tent. Sile, Charikte, and Mother take turns looking after him. I want to sleep. Then it's already morning.

As the day dawns, Charikte begins to prepare himself to make medicine. His preparations will take time, as there are no helpers except Sile. He has so much to do. First he must build a new *dukcha*—a summer dwelling—out of birch bark. But this isn't very difficult. Its door must face the sunrise. Then he must build two fences out of trees—*derpe* and *onang*. There is much to do.

My father sleeps through the day and night. We burn much *kavav* during this time but give him no more whiskey. Then the second day begins. Mother is so exhausted that she's almost ill again. So we have to look after the two of them. When Mother feels better, Charikte continues his preparations, with Sile helping. Then, while our mother sleeps, Father remains quiet, singing from time to time, but calmly. Morso, Tambe, and I—we watch over him. The ropes have cut deeply into his hands and feet. Charikte loosens them but doesn't remove them. If Father is kept tied up like that much longer, his skin will peel off. Even now there is blood on his hands. My heart aches out of pity for him. Why must he suffer so much? Suddenly he opens his eyes and looks us over slowly.

"Father! It's me! Gunilgen!" And I see some understanding in his eyes.

"Daughter," he says, "I am in pain." Morso and I quickly begin to loosen his ropes. He lies quietly. But before we can finish untying the knots, he leaps away from us wildly and his hands are free. He jumps to his feet, drops the ropes, and runs into the wilderness. We are speechless with fear as Father rushes blindly into the forest. Only then do we begin to holler. But it's too late—he has gone, disappearing into the wild.

Hearing our cries, Mother rushes out but slips and falls, having lost all energy. Charikte looks into the forest and is silent. How on earth now are we to bring Father back? He's out of his wits—he can drown, fall off a cliff, or get lost and die. What have we done?!

How long our frustration lasts, I don't know. Suddenly we hear a cuckoo in the forest. "Who's that?" We look at Charikte.

"Don't go after him now," he warns. "We'll only frighten him away. That's him cuckooing. I'll try to get him back."

Turning toward the forest, Charikte answers the call: "Cuck-oo! Cuck-oo!"

And his call is answered: "Cuck-oo!"

"Cuck-oo!" Charikte tries again.

"Cuck-oo! Cuck-oo!" my father answers.

Charikte stands very still while calling, and after a while we can hear the answering "Cuck-oo!" getting closer.

Charikte calls yet again and the cuckooing gets closer still. Soon my father comes out of the trees, cuckooing as if flying toward us. Charikte keeps answering, and Father flies from the trees, still cuckooing, coming toward us. We are too afraid to even move a finger. Then Charikte makes a sign with his head. Mother, it seems, has already prepared the thongs. And finally Father comes toward Charikte, moving not like a human being but a cuckoo bird. Then we all rush him at once, overpowering him and binding him with the thongs. Soon the routine continues as before. We pour whiskey into his mouth and keep him inside the smoky tent.

And father grows quiet.

We finish all the preparations quickly. Charikte has already constructed the *derpe* fencing, which represents the road to the Upper World. It is made from green larch trees cut and laid toward the sunrise. Across this fence Charikte erects a giant image carved from an entire log—the spirit of *calir*, the shaman deer. It will bring Charikte to lands where no human can set foot. We all gather branches for the *onang* fencing, the road to the Lower World. Sile carves birds out of wood—a loon, a duck, a goose, a crane. They will guard the passage to the Lower World and help the shaman protect my father from evil spirits. "Let them keep their watch well," I think to myself. "May my father's soul never pass to the Lower World."

Charikte puts two poles at the end of the *onang* fence. These are the gates to the Middle World, our earth. In front of them he places two wooden fishes—a salmon and a pike. If the evil spirits from the Lower World come to this end of the fence, the fish will swallow them like frogs. Through the smoke-hole of the summerhouse we bring in long thin larch branches. This is the *turu* tree that connects all three worlds and forms a road for Charikte. For Charikte must visit all three worlds. He will fly first to the goddess Ayuikhit-Eni of the Upper World, seeking advice. Then he will step down into the Lower World in search of father's soul, should it be there already. He ties a piece of red cloth to the big tree at the smoke-hole—a present for the spirits of the Upper World, Uga Buga, and a piece of black cloth for the spirits of the Lower World, Hargu Buga. The multicolored strips of cloth are for the spirits of the Middle World, Dulin Buga.

All is ready, it seems. Charikte drinks tea and talks to my mother. Then Mother catches Boy, our deer, purifies him with *kavav* smoke, and ties him to a tree. So Boy will be the offering. He is the offering to save Father.

Evening comes. Charikte cuts down two spears, sharpens the edges, and puts them near the tree where Boy is tied. Mother calls us and says:

"Boy must be sacrificed. Charikte and Sile will do it now. Don't come out of the tent. I'll be right with you."

Sitting in the tent, we hear Charikte and Sile approach Boy. But Boy senses that something is wrong and tries to escape. Then we hear him snort.

"Strike sharply!" Charikte says. "Don't miss!"

Finally, everything is still.

We come out. Boy lies dead, pierced with long spears on each side. Mother, Sile, and Charikte drag him with difficulty to the small *labaz,* the sacred storage hut that Charikte built yesterday. Boy's head is pointed eastward. His eyes are open— big eyes. But they see nothing now.

Suddenly I have no strength in me—my head aches terribly, I feel nauseous, and there are spots before my eyes. I fall down—and keep falling and falling—into darkness. I fly down for a long time, down and down. It gets darker. But where am I flying? "I don't want to go down," I want to say. For down is the Lower World of Hargu Buga. Why would I fly there? Finally, I land and lie somewhere in the darkness. Upward, far, far away, there shines a little star, a spark. I lie for a long time, watching the faraway light. "No! Enough of this," I think. "I must be in the Lower World. I have to get out of here somehow." I step over the sticky clay and find a narrow path. Walk over it. Look around. How poor the land is here! Shrunken yellow grass. Pale dry leaves on small thin trees. And big green grasshoppers everywhere. So many of them! I might have to eat them for food. But look—what's that? There's a fire ahead. Someone must have lit it. An old gray-haired woman sits by the fire. Her clothing is ancient and strange.

"What is the source of your blood-root?" she asks me.

"You should know that yourself, Grandmother," I answer. "For you must be the one who keeps the road to the Lower World."

"Yes, that's me. And I'm asking you because I shouldn't let you in. Just yesterday I didn't let your father's soul pass. Both of you have come here ahead of your time."

"And is my father's soul back to earth already?"

"It is. And now you must go back, too. But wait a minute—do you see the sparks from my fire? There is Paskene's spark among them. There it is—the brightest and the biggest. Catch it and take it with you back to Earth."

And with my hand I catch the biggest and brightest spark, clutch it tightly, and go back along the road. The spark burns my hand, but I keep my fist shut so it won't get away. I will bring it back to Earth, and my father will become a *nimnakanlan,* a singer of tales. Suddenly, I hear singing from afar. Singing to the sound of a drum. The voice seems familiar. Oh, it's Charikte, and that's his drum! He is calling me back with his singing and his drum. From this world to the Middle Earth of Dulin Buga. Now he sings, now he cries like a crane. And suddenly that spot of light broadens above. Out of it appears a long chain, swinging, lowering down toward me. Closer and closer it comes. Now I see a big hook at its end. The hook catches my body and the chain carries me upward. I come closer and closer to the spot of light. Suddenly, with great force the chain is pulled from the hole, and the hole closes down. . . .

I open my eyes. Mother, pale and drawn, looks at me and cries out in joy:

"Oh, Mother Ayuikhit-Eni. My little tomtit bird is back home on Earth again! Bless us!"

She gives me tea, raising my head a little. I drink and look around, searching the tent with my eyes. My father is sleeping, and I look at my mother with questioning eyes.

"All is well," she says. "Father is home, too. He just fell asleep. Both of you almost stayed in the Lower World."

"I had the spark of Granddaddy Paskene in my hand, mother. Did you see it?" And I tell her everything I saw down below.

"Yes, yes, I did," she answers. "The spark now lives in your father's heart. He is recovering, and tomorrow he will begin telling his first *nimnakan*."

(

And for seven long days we listen to my father's *nimnakans*. How did he learn them? I wonder. Ah! It was because of Granddaddy Paskene. Through his spark the *nimnakans* came to my father.

She hadn't been back to her native grounds for a long time. And now she was returning for good. For almost fifteen years she'd been away from home, living in the Ukraine, having married a *hohol* from "Hohland" as he called himself, making fun of the traditional Ukrainian haircut, the shaven head with a single lock—a *hohol*—left on top.

She was returning alone, without her son. He wouldn't let her take their son, who had come to resemble his father. He'd inherited nothing from her—not the eyes, not the nose, not the color of his hair. At times she couldn't believe he was really her son. Her mother-in-law loved the grandson and was happy he didn't take after his mother. The more he'd grown, the more alienated from her he'd become. She had tried once to teach him some Evenk words, but even his tongue was constructed in such a way that it could pronounce properly only what came from Hohland.

With every passing year she'd been drawn more and more to her own homeland. Her husband wouldn't vacation with her there or even let her go by herself, so her life had become more and more miserable. Still, she would have remained patient for the sake of her son, but then her husband finally told her that he was sick of her. Having said so, he married another woman and took the son with him. So now she was going home. Where else could she go?

After flying into Blagoveschensk, she couldn't fly farther out to Zeya for a long time. The weather was bad and her money was running low. But finally the weather improved and she made it. Seeing the familiar regional airport again, she nearly burst into tears. As a girl she'd gone there often—for amateur concerts and sports competitions, for she was good on skis. She even took part once in a regional essay contest, winning a prize for a story about her grandpa. But all of this had happened so long ago, to the point of disbelief.

She had very little money left, and she went about the airport in Zeya hoping to find a familiar face with slanted eyes. And she found one—actually three—two aging men and a woman. Approaching them, she was so afraid that her tongue wouldn't be able to utter any Native words that she began to stammer, asking in Evenk, "Who are you?"

The eldest of the three, almost an old man, laughed and said, "Can't an Evenk even recognize an Evenk? What kind of blood runs in your veins? Where is your blood-root?"

And suddenly she began to cry.

"Oh," he said, "if you cry too much your eyes will dry out. Sit down." He moved a little, giving her some room.

Her skirt was too short to let her sit the way they did, so she sat on her haunches beside them.

"Are you from the vicinity? Whose daughter are you?"

"I'm from Bomnak, the daughter of Yepelken and Ogdo, of the Markov family."

"I knew them," the man answered. "We're from Bryanta, but I knew your kin."

"Where are you flying to?"

"Dambuki, along the river, and home to Bryanta. I came for my old woman. She's been in the hospital. Had an operation. They had to cut something out of her, but she'll live now."

"You're an old man yourself," his wife interrupted, "and I'm not an old woman—I'm fifteen years younger than you! If I want, I could marry Apana here." She flashed her dark eyes and elbowed the man sitting next to her. Then she asked, "What's your name? Where are you coming from? How long have you been away?"

"My name is Barbara." She thought and corrected herself: "I am Balba." Then she began to tell them about herself.

They listened in silence, never interrupting, now and then sighing or shaking their heads, until Barbara stopped talking and began crying again.

"It's okay, daughter," said Sogdekon, the elderly man. "The only bad thing is that you've given away your son. Mother's blood always prevails, so it must have been your own fault. Perhaps when you nursed him you didn't think about your kin. He has sucked your milk—how come he's not Evenk?"

"I didn't even come home to bury my father," Barbara blurted, sobbing again.

Sogdekon's wife gave a bright look. "My! My! The water's rising in the river again. And to think of it, there's been no rain!"

Barbara looked at her, puzzled. There was no river nearby. Then she met the merry eyes of the woman and smiled, holding back her tears.

"Do you have any money?" Sogdekon asked.

"Next to nothing."

"Stolen?" his wife asked quickly. "You know, yesterday my old man almost parted with his own because of a wicked man. If it weren't for me, we'd be broke!"

"No, we wouldn't," Sogdekon replied. "Your own money's hidden away."

"I'm different!" she said, waving her hand. "I don't carry money in my pocket. And nobody's going to find my stash."

"Remember how they stole your handbag in Dambuki?"

"No big deal. Just trinkets inside. But you didn't hide your money, so it was stolen. Remember? By my girlfriend! We talked and walked with her for three hours, and she was so nice—and then she stole it! Went away with the bag. For good, and didn't leave her address, although she had said earlier, 'I'll give you my address. You should come visit!'" The woman laughed. "But I have no regrets. Let her steal. She won't prosper, nor have a clean face because of it. But her insides will rot, right, Balba?"

She talked some more, and when the men went to inquire about the flights, she began to talk about herself.

"Everyone calls me Nyraikan. My man does, too. But on my passport I am Evdokiya, because I was very small when they arranged for me to be Sogdekon's wife. That's how it was in the old days—husband and wife were assigned from childhood. So it was with me. Right after birth I was intended to be his wife. My mother died when I was barely a year old, and I became an orphan. So Sogdekon's parents adopted me. His mother fed me, and Sogdekon himself cared for me. That's why I'm Nyraikan—his child. I can't say a bad word about him: he raised me from the crib and spoiled me with his attention. Even now he treats me like a child. When the time came, we were married. Oh, but I'll tell you! Want to hear the story of how I became his wife?" Her eyes flashed like a small, cunning girl's.

"At it again, Nyraikan?" Sogdekon said, overhearing his wife as he approached. "Daughter, don't listen to everything she says. Let her words go in one ear and out the other, or your head will crack. When we get home, I'm going to take Nyraikan to the mountains with her girlfriends and leave them with the magpies. You'll become their leader," he said to his wife. He took out a bundle with food and handed it to her. "Well, you should eat, magpie."

"And where's the tea?" his wife asked. "You can't have food without tea. We must have tea."

"Where's the canteen?" Sogdekon asked. "I'll go get tea."

"Couldn't you have brought your own? You know all too well I can't eat in the canteen," Nyraikan joked. "The people get in my way."

The exchange brightened Barbara. This is how a wife should talk to her husband, she thought. And what did I get from my own husband? Just "Bring me this" or "Get me that." What a fool I was.

Sogdekon brought tea, gave it to the women, then returned to Apana who was standing near the gate.

"Let's drink tea and talk," Nyraikan said with satisfaction. "Why is Apana so gloomy?"

"Oh," sighed Nyraikan, "he's alone now. His wife died here, in the hospital. We were in there together. What a disaster! She was so young, and if it weren't for this lousy sea, she wouldn't have died."

"The Zeya Sea, or the reservoir?"

"Oh my, what life has brought! The sea itself. Truly, man always wants more and more. He has spoiled the earth, destroyed the game, and created rotten seas. Look at the sea for yourself when you fly. How can you call it a sea? It's just a dead swamp, with black tree stubs sticking out everywhere. Only big pike, like huge logs, live in it. Yet you shouldn't catch them—people are getting poisoned from these pike. Even in the rivers nearby it's dangerous to fish.

"Well, Apana's wife went to see his son, who lives with the Russians in the town of Sneznogorsk. His wife is Russian and they're happy together. Once, they ate smoked fish from the sea. It was okay for the Russians; they have no problem with it. The pollutants don't affect them. But we're accustomed to fresh food. Who knows? Maybe we have different stomachs. She ate some of that fish and got sick. They brought her here to Zeya, and she died here. Poisoned, they say. Everyone else who ate it was okay, but she got poisoned. Why only she? It must be true that our stomachs are different from the Russians'. And so Apana's alone now. He's stayed a long time, because he buried his wife here. Spent the entire summer near the cemetery, in the forest. Now he's decided to go home with us. He's still young, just a little over fifty. And how old are you?"

"Thirty-three."

"Well, you'll get your life in order still. Marry one of your own kin, and you'll be all right."

Apana came up and stared wistfully out the window into the sky. "They say a plane is flying to Dambuki after lunch, so we'll go today." Having announced the news, he went off and sat by Sogdekon.

"I grew up happily in Sogdekon's family," Nyraikan continued. "There was no one to harm me. And truly, in the old days, they didn't harm the women much. Of course, some educated people say that life was hard for the Evenk women, but when has life ever been easy? Just being alive is always difficult. It's even harder for the men, for everything always depends on them—whether you eat or not, whether the deer survive.

"Sogdekon was a brother to me, and a father as well. He was already mature. He hunted and owned his own deer. His mother taught me how to keep house, how to sew and embroider, how to get in food for the future. I was a daughter to her. She died when I was ten. Sogdekon's father had died earlier, so we were left alone. I knew how to do almost everything. But when he'd go off hunting, I'd forget all my chores and begin to play. I'd play with the dogs and forget to cook dinner. So he'd come home, cook the dinner himself, and feed me. When we went to bed, I'd be afraid, and I'd come to him. Once, he started to touch my breasts. They had just begun to grow, to tighten up. You know how they hurt when they grow. So he would touch them, and I'd say, 'Don't do that. They even hurt by themselves. When will they grow and stop hurting?'

" 'They'll stop all right,' he'd answer. 'You just grow up well, and don't fall ill, please.'

"In winter he'd always carry me to the enclosed sledge, so I wouldn't get my feet wet. And that's how we lived. I remember it well—it was March, and he'd gone after squirrels. For two days I was at home waiting for him, doing my chores. By then I knew how to do everything, for I was almost fifteen. His mother had died a long time ago, so she never had time to tell me about women's problems. I was too young then. But when migrating, we met people, women among them, of course, but I never thought to ask. And so I knew nothing about being a woman. When Sogdekon went hunting, he took just two of the deer; the rest stayed home. I cooked some dinner for myself, ate, and went out to relieve myself.

"Well, the deer liked to lick salt, and they usually licked urine in the snow. So when I left the tent, one buck came right over, waiting for me. I sat down to urinate and saw blood in the snow. I was frightened because I couldn't account for the blood. I fell down in the snow, desperate. Should I cry, or call Sogdekon for help? The buck came closer, sniffed the blood, and refused to lick it. That's when I really grew frightened—I must be in trouble and would probably die. From women's talk I had heard that you could lose all your blood and die. So I went back into the tent, lay on my bed, and waited for Sogdekon. He returned in the evening. The stove was out, it was cold in the tent, and no tea or food was ready.

" 'What happened to you?' he said. 'Are you ill?'

"And in a flash he began to feed the stove and put on tea. My stomach ached, as if cut with a knife, but I just lay there and said nothing.

" 'Where does it hurt?' Sogdekon asked.

"I was ashamed to tell him. How could I tell him where the blood was coming from? I didn't know the word. Well, I thought, I'm going to die, and Sogdekon will be left alone. Pitying him, I said, 'You've done so much to care for me and raise me, but you won't see me become your wife, for I'm sick and I'm going to die.'

" 'Please tell me what's wrong with you,' he said.

"But I kept silent. Then I doubled up from a new spasm of pain. Sogdekon came up and said, 'Let me look at your stomach—is it soft or tight? What have you been eating?'

" 'Nothing you didn't eat as well. Don't look at my stomach—it's soft all right.'

"But hunters have a good nose for scents; he must have smelled the blood.

"'Oh, you are truly like my own child,' he said, 'growing up away from women, alone. But you know, all girls start to have that. You will make me a wife soon.'

"'What!' I said. 'I'll lose all my blood and die! Are you laughing at me? You'd better think of a way to stop the blood. Listen to me—I'm going to die!'

"'I'll cure you soon,' he said.

"He made a concoction from some herbs and gave it to me. 'Drink this,' he smiled, 'and it'll go away in three days.'

"He boiled some water, brought some clean cloths, and went out so that I might wash myself. I did, and I put some cloth inside me, so it was difficult to walk. But it became easier, my spirits lifted, and I forgot about dying.

"'As soon as this goes,' I told Sogdekon, 'I'll become your wife. I'll leave my girl's bedding right here, at this camp.'

"'You may very well leave your bed behind,' he said, 'but you need to grow a little more. Your bones are not yet those of a woman. They are childish, so our children would be weak. Let's wait one more year. And your breasts aren't big enough yet. For we need not just one child but many. If I make you my wife right now, you'll stop growing and your bones will stay as they are. You might have problems giving birth, because your thighs are still girlish.'

"'All right,' I said. 'You know best. Let me stay your child or sister for one more year.'

"'Next year, at the beginning of summer, I'll gather what relatives we have left. Meanwhile, you can begin to sew things for the marriage.'

"'Oh, but I already have two marriage bags. I sewed them without telling you. I have two big carpets, the *kumulans*. Let's announce our wedding tomorrow. Those who must give me gifts, according to the law of relations, need time to prepare them for the occasion.'

"I was so happy that I sprang from my bed and began to prepare food, to check my sewing kit, thinking about things yet to be made.

" 'Oh, imagine, in this condition it's possible to walk and work—just think of it! And I was afraid I'd bleed to death.'

"Sogdekon laughed at my words. And of all the children he received from me, the first was the most painful. I couldn't deliver it for a long time. If he had made me his wife earlier, I couldn't have done it at all. It was hard, even two years after my first period. I had seven children in all, and four are still living. Three died early, from childhood diseases. They were spaced every three years, and they fed on my milk for two years. As soon as I finished nursing, I was expecting another baby. We lived well with Sogdekon. My job was to give birth and nurse the infants. And as soon as they were on their feet, he took over. Yes, Sogdekon loved his children, all right! We had only sons. Two are with us at Bryanta now. Two others are grown, educated, and live in big cities—one in Blagoveschensk, another in Krasnoyarsk. They visit us and invite us to visit them, but we're content at home. My old man is sturdy. We still keep deer—we have sixteen. Our elder son is looking after them right now. And my son-in-law is nice, too."

"How could you have a son-in-law? You said you only had sons."

"Well, we adopted a girl, an orphan. One of our women had a baby with a Russian, then died. So we took the child. Oh, my son-in-law is as good as can be. It's just that his tribe has such a funny name. The way it's pronounced, it sounds like name-calling, and I don't like that."

"Who is he?"

"Don't laugh, please. He's a good man, all right, however you look at him. But—well, you know what we call the most manly part of a man? That's his name—Kakas."

Barbara laughed, offending Nyraikan. "I knew you'd laugh!" she said. "But what can you do if that's his name?"

Barbara stifled her laughter with great difficulty. "Is he a Khakas?" she asked, pronouncing it with a silent *h*. "From the Khakas people? One of those ethnic Turks from the upper Yenisei River?" She started laughing again.

"You wonder why they gave him such a name. As soon as I tell anyone about him, they start laughing. A disaster! Yet he's such a nice man, despite the name of his tribe. Who could have offended them so. We Evenks are different. We'd never give a good person a name like that."

Sogdekon came up to them hurriedly. "There's a plane's ready for Bomnak," he said, panting. He took out some money, counted enough for a ticket, then added twenty rubles more. Having arranged the bills in his hand, he gave them to Barbara.

"Fly home, daughter. Run quickly, or they'll leave without you."

There were already ten people in line waiting to board the little plane—one middle-aged Russian woman and nine gold miners whose team worked near Bomnak. No Evenks were among them. All the miners were tipsy, and seeing Barbara coming for a ticket, they stared at her rudely. The tickets were sold rapidly and boarding was announced. Then the Russian woman ran from the airport building, carrying a big sack containing a screeching piglet. Barbara followed.

"Hurry up!" urged a young woman in an Aeroflot uniform. "There's always a problem with these Bomnak passengers!"

Everyone followed her. Barbara wanted to say good-bye to her new friends but was afraid to fall behind the others. Then her friends appeared, running toward her, beyond the railing where it was prohibited to go. She waved frantically, and then she heard Sogdekon.

"If it goes badly for you," he called, "come to us!"

"I have a cousin," Nyraikan cried, smiling. "We'll marry you to him!"

Having boarded the plane, Barbara settled into her seat and began to observe the other passengers. The pig screeched endlessly. The Russian woman struck him with her hand. "What a pest!" she scolded.

"Slaughter it fast!" joked one of the miners. "Or I'll go deaf!"

"We don't keep pigs at home," the woman explained, "so I had to go to town to buy one. I'm tired of him myself. Would you shut up, you dirty little pig?"

But the little pig wouldn't stop screeching, so the woman started to rock him to sleep like a baby. Meanwhile, the plane was gaining altitude, flying over the reservoir. The co-pilot looked in from the cockpit, smiled at the woman, and closed the door again.

"He knows me," the woman said. "My son works in Blagoveschensk as an airplane mechanic. So they know my son well." She sounded glad.

The pig cried louder.

"*Utchune!*" the woman cried back.

Barbara wanted to laugh; the woman was trying to hush the pig in Evenk.

"*Utchune!* Hush!" she said again, and for some reason the pig quieted down. "What a beast! He doesn't understand Russian but knows Evenk in a flash!"

She spoke loudly in order to be heard. Then she looked out the window and made a face. "What a waste they've made of this place! We're lucky this sea doesn't come close to us! But these guys—" She looked at the miners, then moved closer to Barbara and whispered in her ear. "They mine gold up the Zeya River. The water's so muddy now you can't wash your linen! How beautiful it used to be!"

She shouted something else, but Barbara closed her eyes,

not listening, just nodding her head. The air was bumpy, for the sea was choppy. Yet Barbara managed to nap.

Later, when she stepped down from the plane, she noticed the changes immediately—trees had grown up near the lonely airport building, and a new green fence had appeared. The airport looked alien, not as she remembered it.

"Are you looking for someone?" said the woman with the pig. "I don't seem to remember you."

"I don't remember you either. I haven't been here for fifteen years."

"No wonder I don't recognize you. I've been living in Bomnak for thirteen years. Before that I lived in Ogoron. Then they dismantled the place, so I came here. And now, they say, they're going to reopen it again. Who did you come to see?"

"My aunt lives here, Nyura Hisuni."

"Oh, my," the woman cried out. "She died last spring!"

"No! I wrote her last winter that I might come."

"She fell ill quickly and was gone in three months. Cancer. I wonder how people get cancer. And her Nikolay, when she died, went fishing in his boat and was drowned. On the fortieth day after the funeral, when the soul of the departed leaves the earth for good. It's lucky they found him. He washed ashore on a piece of driftwood. Had he been driven out into this rotten sea, he'd have been lost. The pike would have eaten him. They're big as logs out there."

The airport was two miles from the village. They went along the little path down a hill. The sack with the pig was heavy, and the woman's arms ached. The pig was either asleep or resigned to its fate.

After they had walked about a kilometer the woman said, "We're about to pass the cemetery. Let's sit and rest a bit." She sat down on the ground, and as she lowered the sack the pig stirred, then started screeching again. "*Utchune!*" she cried again. "You must *utchune!* The people here are at rest." She sighed. "Ah, after fifteen years, many people would be gone. Who are your parents?"

"I'm the daughter of Yepelken and Ogdo, from the Markov family."

"Oh my god!" the woman cried again and looked at her carefully. "Yepelken died five years ago. What a pity. He was a good man. Why didn't you come for the funeral? Well, we had it without you, all right. I don't know what became of his deer—they must be with his nephew, Yegor. Your father lived and hunted in the taiga forest until he died. He brought me two good sables once, to be sent to his daughter. That would be you, then. But I'm as illiterate as you, so I said to him, ask one of the young people, they can write. But I never asked him who sent the sables. Did you ever get them?"

"Yes," Barbara said. "But do you know where my father's grave is?"

"Of course. I tossed a handful of earth on his coffin. Do you want to see it right now?"

"Just show it to me, please, and then go home."

"Let's go, and I'll show you. And you stop screeching there," she said to the pig, lifting her sack to her back. "One should be *utchune* here!"

As always, the cemetery was quiet, the graves set evenly among the trees. As they approached, Barbara put her bag down quickly, as if remembering something. Searching it, she took out two new rolls of cloth. She tore the edge with her teeth and ripped several strips from one, then the other. Then she searched her bag again, took out a pack of cigarettes, and began smoking.

"Show me the grave, please," she said, adding quietly, for some reason, "my mother's is far away in the taiga."

The woman went forward, leaving the pig in the sack. Then she stopped. "That's where your father lives now. And there's nobody to put a fence around his grave. It's good you've come.

We can fence it in later. Well, I'll be going now. Sit and talk with your father."

And she was gone.

Barbara fastened the strips of cloth to the cross, lit another cigarette, and put it on the grave. The smoke lingered in the air, as if her father, having not smoked for so long, was happy to be doing so again.

(

When she neared the village, Barbara spotted the familiar house. Tanya, her childhood friend, lived there. And if Tanya had moved, at least her mother would still be there. They had never exchanged letters. From the moment Barbara left for school and married her *hohol,* she'd stopped writing to all her friends. But occasionally she wrote to Auntie Nyura, inquiring about her father.

She came to the porch, but there was a lock on the door. Oh my god, she thought. Who should I visit? She lingered at the edge of the village. Yegor is in the taiga, caring for the deer. He doesn't live in the village. Where should I go? Ah, well, she thought. I'll go along the street and see what happens. I might meet someone.

New houses stood at the edge of the village where the forest used to be. They were big homes, for two families. Barbara went along the street. Children were playing behind the fence of one of the houses, taking turns riding a bicycle. Seeing her, they came to the fence and stared through the slats. A boy of six thrust his head through the fence and asked, "Auntie, who have you come to see?"

Two girls, younger than the boy, approached and stared at her also.

"Auntie, who have you come to see?"

Barbara didn't know what to say. Instead, she asked, "And what is your mother's name?"

"Our mother is Moskalyan's Auntie Valya," the boy said.

"And your father?"

"Moskalyan."

"Moskalyan?" Barbara tried to remember the name from the old days. The children were of mixed blood, therefore their mother was Evenk. Barbara searched her mind for girls with that name—Valya Trifonova, Valya Sofronova, Valya Kolesova. Damn! she thought. Sometimes these mixed bloods are so unlike their parents there's no way to tell whose children they are.

The door of the house opened and a voice crossed the porch. "Oh you, devils! Moskalyan's children! Why are you home from kindergarten so early?"

Barbara recognized the voice. It was Valentina Trifonova—Valya—but her voice was piercing and unpleasant.

"Pests! Who let you out so early?" Valentina asked, coming out to the porch.

The children turned at their mother's voice but stayed at the fence. When Valentina noticed Barbara, she kept silent, though it was clear she had more to say. Stepping from the porch, she walked to the fence and said in a loud and amazed voice, "Is that you, Barbara? Yes, it's Balba! What wind has blown you our way?"

"I just came," Barbara replied.

"Come on in, don't just stand there like that!"

Barbara entered the yard through the gate of the fence.

"Go and see your grandma!" Valentina ordered the children.

And only then did it become clear to Barbara that Valentina was tipsy. They went onto the porch as the children ran off to their grandma.

"I was just thinking," Valentina said, "who should I drink with? You're just in time. Let's drink to your coming!" She took a three-liter can of homemade spirits from under the table. "We make it ourselves now," she laughed. "And it tastes like it!"

"Who's your husband?" Barbara asked. "What a strange name."

"Moskalyan—he's from Moldova. He came to us a long time ago, without a passport, living in hiding. Now he has papers. He's away at the moment, prospecting for gold up the Zeya River with a team of miners."

"Did you graduate from college?"

"Oh, I graduated all right—one of the best. Yet in the winter I work stoking stoves. In summer I wash floors at the farm office."

"Why not use your education?"

"Who would take me? After I graduated, there were no jobs. I worked at the animal farm, feeding the foxes, scientifically. May they all die out! Other positions— animal technician, veterinarian—were all taken. Such possibilities weren't for us. Oh, so many years have passed"—she waved her hand—"I've forgotten my studies. My education was good for nothing. At college they directed me to the cow farm. I went but didn't like it there. I'm afraid of cows. I'd prefer deer. For several years I waited for a position that suited my training. I'm still waiting.

"Do you remember Yuri Liandau? When we were still in school he came here. Since he'd already graduated from agricultural college, he was given a position. He was fat even then, but you should see him now! So I'm jobless, and that's how I live. Then I married Moskalyan, even though I knew he didn't have a passport. But one has to do something! You messed up your own life, too—Auntie Nyura told me—you live poorly and want to come back. Where's your son?"

"With his father."

"For good, right?"

Barbara was silent.

"So he won't let you have him? Well, you're less lucky than I was. You didn't come back for so many years—what a beast your husband must be! But me—I don't give in to Moskalyan. Just give him a blow with anything I can lay my hands on, and he stops at once. But you—you were always a coward in school. You never fought anybody. See this bruise on my leg?" She raised her dress to show it. "The idiot! Well, I hit him with a bottle. I doubt his head's in one piece now."

"You could have killed him."

"What else is he good for?" Valentina was indifferent. "He beat me a year ago, and I almost died. He got what was coming to him."

"How can you live like that?"

"Did you live any better? Never coming home in fifteen years, not even to bury your father? That tells you something. Although your man didn't beat you, he kept you in his grip. You were worthless in his eyes. Me, at least I fight back. You couldn't even do that."

A gloomy silence fell. Barbara didn't respond.

"So what of it, Balba?" Valentina was drunk now, very drunk. "Forget it. You've come home." She refilled the glasses, they drank, and Barbara began to feel tipsy herself.

"Let's go see Zina. She'll be happy to see you. Her life's a mess, too, just like ours."

"I'm not going anywhere," Barbara said, barely able to move her tongue. The drink was strong.

"Well, let's stay then. Let's dance. Come on—I'll put a record on. My favorite—" She could barely pronounce her words.

Shakily, they made it into the house. Valentina turned on the record player and a melody of their student years filled the room. She began to dance as the record player roared: "Once again the last train's run away from me . . ."

"By the railroad tracks again," Valentina sang loudly, "by the railroad tracks again!" She tore a long, wide screen from the window and started to dance with it crazily. "Those tracks came on their own," she sang in a drunken voice. "They made the road all right, right near here, with all the tracks! With all the tracks!" Getting tangled in the screen, she fell to the floor and began to laugh. "The devil! Everything's run away from me! My whole life's run off somewhere!"

Barbara fell on the sofa and passed out. It was five in the evening.

(

A loud knock at the door brought Barbara to her senses. It was dark in the room. She found the light switch with difficulty and pushed it. Valentina was asleep beside her, on the floor. Groggy, she awoke. "Who's breaking down the door?" she said. "How can anyone get any sleep around here?" She went to open the door.

Barbara sat down on the sofa, trying to make herself presentable. What a shame, she thought bitterly, to get drunk at the very first house, even though it's with a girlfriend. But to drink like a pig! People will think I'm always like this.

She found a comb and ran it through her hair.

"Nadya! How good of you to come!" Valentina's happy voice sounded from the door. "Do come in, do come in! Are you going to scold me again? It's all right this time—I haven't been drinking alone, but with Balba Markova. Do you remember her? She's come home, for good." Valentina returned to the room with her guest.

Barbara recognized her—it was Nadya Sologon. They greeted each other, Barbara ashamed of her own appearance.

"Well, you sure had a good time, girls," Nadya said, lifting the screen from the floor. "Why'd you tear the screen from the window?"

"Ah, well—" Valentina waved her hand. "I was in the mood to dance. I took the screen for no reason and got tangled in it. Then I fell down and slept on the floor. Balba was more intelligent—she slept on the sofa. We drank like pigs."

"Pigs don't get drunk," Nadya said. "Put on some tea. I'd like some. What were you drinking? Spirits?"

"Homemade—you know we have prohibition here. My stuff is strong," Valentina said. "Two glasses and we were off our feet. Did you bring us a present from Baikal-Amur?"

"If I'd known you had something to drink, I wouldn't have bothered. Please, Valentina, find me something to eat. I haven't eaten yet, I had so many things to attend to. I had a bite or two with Auntie Uliena, and that was it."

"You Sologons sure have learned to live with the Russians," Valentina said. "It was hard for your parents, but easy for you now. You Sologons have character. You're almost Russian. There's truth to that old saying 'Great harm always brings a little good.' Weren't your parents against the collective farms? Now you get along better than the Evenks. You're domineering, too, minding your own business, just like the Russians."

"I'm not like them at all," Nadya replied. "My face sticks out in a crowd. And let me tell you—why should I have a child with an Evenk, knowing it'll have a hard life? I had a daughter with a Belogur guy. If you add some Russian character to her beauty, life will be easier for her. How many Evenks are left? Next to none. If we have children with our own kind, we're just spoiling their lives. I know this sounds horrible, because I'm Evenk and my parents are Evenks, but I think it's better this way. As the educated say, we're not the 'surviving kind.' Education gets us nowhere."

"You're right," Valentina added. They were talking education now. "Just count how many of us got an education, yet there are no jobs around. Rita Buta came here from Potekhino. She couldn't make it there, and after two or three mistakes in her classroom, she lost her credentials as a Russian teacher. She's physically too weak to stand up for her rights, so she came here. And there's no job for her.

"Zina Denme graduated from Leningrad University, but all she's allowed to do is supervise student homework. She used to teach at the Evenk elementary school, but now that's over.

They closed the school. They reasoned that since Evenk children don't know Russian very well, they should start it in the early grades. Even the high school students confuse the endings and gender. That's true, but what can you do without your own native tongue?

"Agnia managed to keep her teaching job for three years, then was transferred to a boarding school because a new teacher arrived who doesn't confuse genders. The boarding school directors change every year. They're all newcomers, with no credibility.

"And what about me? There was no way I'd get that vet position. And who'd hire me now, if this Liandau goes? My reputation's shot—I'm drinking too much. But would it have come to that, if I had started working when I got my degree? If you're not treated as a human being from the beginning, how can you become one later?

"Sasha Likhanov graduated from an aviation technology college, spent four years at Blagoveschensk—a major city—and wound up here. The taiga called him. He's a hunter now. His heart's not in flying. Who can explain it? Who's to blame? Us? Somebody else? Why'd we bother to study? You're right, Nadya. It's no use having Evenk children. They'll become martyrs, just like us."

"We better have a drink." Nadya put a bottle on the table. "I've brought you some dry wine."

They poured it and drank. Then they heard footsteps on the porch, a knock at the door, and a young Evenk woman entered.

"Valya," she said, "please give me the medicine I asked about."

Valentina brought out the medicine, gave it to her, and the woman left. Then she sat down, lost in thought. Pouring more wine, she said suddenly, "Listen, Nadya. I was foolish to suggest you should marry Tolya Kolesov. You're probably related."

"Maybe, but distantly."

"I don't know—it happened with Leonid and Olga."

"What? I don't remember her. Was that her at the door just now?"

"Yes. She was very small when we were in school. You remember Leonid? He was a little younger than us."

"Yes—he limped. Later, he disappeared."

"He was put into the TB clinic in Blagoveschensk. He finished school there, then went to a visual arts college. He draws really well. He returned some time ago. Olga had no parents. She was an orphan, like Leonid. Nobody knew they were together, and when they did, it was too late. The grandmothers discovered they're related. But they got married, and then the trouble came—their child was born all wrong. Its head is too big. He's a year old now but can't hold his head upright. They say he won't last long. Speaking of distant relations . . ."

Barbara finally spoke up. "If you look deep enough into our family trees, everyone in Bomnak's related. And we all die out. When my mother was alive, she used to say that all the boys were related, either closely or distantly. She always wanted to go to Zolotinka in Yakutia, because there are Evenk people there—to find me a husband. She died fearing I'd never find an Evenk husband. Yet by Evenk law, only seventh-generation relatives can marry."

"Who can tell the generations apart?" Valentina asked. "There are no old men or women left. Pretty soon we'll all intermarry and die out."

"It's the same with the deer," Nadya said. "When we lived alone, our herd was small. When all the Evenks joined the collective farms, we were the only ones to stay on separate land, south of Dambuki. We had just one bull, and if we got a younger one, he was of the same blood, so in time the young ones stopped giving birth. And if they did, they died out. We're just like the deer. We may be people, but we're a part of nature all the same. What's the difference—man or insect? We all have to continue, so life will go on. I remember a proverb my father used to repeat: 'The Earth bears everything; a human being's but a tiny particle.' He meant that everything on Earth is connected—people, environment, beasts. Yet I interpret it differently—we're insignificant, mere trifles, pine needles. That's what we've become."

They chattered some more, then turned to Barbara.

"Well, you've come home," Valentina said. "And have you thought about work? Do you think you'll find a job? We need janitors here. One full-time job at the state farm is divided among two or three people, so that our boys can have some sort of work. Women work half-time, because there aren't enough jobs."

"I haven't given it much thought. Couldn't I find something else?"

"No way," Valentina said. "Lusia Puyagir came back last winter, and she's still unemployed. Where would you work? All positions at the state farm are taken. Same at the canteen. They only need three people in forestry, and they're already there. A nurse—to wash toilets at the kindergarten and the clinic—that's taken, too. I don't know how you can earn a living here. Maybe Nadya could find you something at Baikal-Amur?"

"We have a need for manual labor," Nadya said, "but you have to be strong. It's difficult for women to get jobs, but you could look around. Some of our girls tried it but had to quit."

"That was sheer comedy," Valentina replied. "Remember how our girls went to work in Zeya? Valya Uchiki and Rimma Chokoty found jobs there. 'Look at our smart girls,' everyone said. 'They've found employment in the big city! Now we can go and visit them!' I went to Zeya once, to see my daughter in the hospital, and guess what? The girls were digging holes and planting trees along the streets.

"Well, Valya Uchiki is sturdy enough—the dirt was flying from her shovel. But Rimma is small and thin, and the shovel was too big for her. She could hardly lift it. Everyone stared at them. Rimma felt awkward. She wanted to hide in the hole she was digging, but she couldn't dig it deep enough. Valya was so mad she threw dirt at the passersby, and they got angry. Who wouldn't? You know how long they lasted? Until the second paycheck. They got drunk to numb the pain and didn't show up for work the next day. So they got fired. That's their story. To top it off, they're both rather unattractive. Look at their nick-names—*Uchiki,* the lame one, and *Chokoty,* the bent one. Our two Misses Evenk, the best we had, went job hunting in Zeya. There was only shame, nothing more."

"Not quite," Nadya said. "I've just transported some perishable produce here from Zeya—milk, sour cream, and vegetables. I documented it, loaded it on the plane, and we were ready to go. Then I went into the canteen for a snack, and guess who was there? Valya and Rimma! They were drinking tea, and they were happy to see me. It was after lunch. The regular plane for Bomnak flies earlier in the morning, once a day only. So Valya said to me, 'Ask the pilots if we can fly among the cabbages and potatoes. Take us to Bomnak, or to Verhnezeysk, and we'll go the rest of the way by boat.'

" 'But aren't you working?' I asked. 'We have to go today,' Uchiki said, 'or we'll get hurt.'

" 'What happened?' I said.

" 'We were staying at a hostel,' Uchiki said. 'We got paid yesterday and had a party, drinking a little. One man approached Rimma rather crudely, so I beat him up. I wanted to knife him. But he was too small and he was drunk, so I just beat him up and we ran from the hostel. We couldn't get plane tickets this morning—we've just been waiting here. If that guy finds us, he'll kill us. We have to leave quickly.'

" 'What about your job?' I said. 'Your documents? Can you go without them?'

" 'To hell with them,' Rimma said. 'We haven't done much

here. We'll be happy just to get out in one piece. He'll kill us, you know.'

"And that's the story," Nadya said. "I didn't have much cargo to take, so we agreed on the flight. The waves were high on the sea, so the ride was bumpy. But the girls braced themselves against the potato cases and flew happily. I think Uchiki totally forgot about that man she feared so much. That's how they got here. And today, when I was walking through the streets, I met Valya. Is she strong or what? She was carrying a heavy sack on her shoulders like a purse, strolling right along with it. I didn't know what was inside, or what she might have done, but she saw me and was happy.

" 'Well,' she said, her fists flying, 'didn't I teach that guy something?'

" 'Are you threatening me,' I joked.

" 'No,' she said. 'I just wanted to teach someone else a lesson!'

"Then she went on her way. And as she left, I saw Rimma running after her."

(

The young women sat for a long time, remembering friends and growing sadder. A decent life was the exception. They didn't sleep until morning, then Nadya left for her office, and Barbara decided to freshen up to visit in the village.

She followed the familiar street, and there was the little social hall. It was the same, only older and more dilapidated. But there was a new fence around it. It was difficult not to go into the yard and through the little gate. Wooden planks ran from the gate to the club entrance, some of them new. The surrounding trees had grown up, the birches were tall, and it was quiet and shady. It was here in the old days that she used to go to see movies or attend dances. She drew close to the walls and lightly touched the blackened timber. Then she saw the inscription

carved into the planks with a knife. *Bomnak—Little America.*
The words were underlined.

Who on earth could have written this? she thought.

The ironic inscription stuck in her mind, and she sat down
on a bench under the birches to think about it. Little America?

A while later she got up and went to the local store. Auntie
Darya was sitting on the porch. The store opened at ten, but it
was only nine-thirty. Auntie Darya was already an old woman.
What had happened to the strong woman she used to be?

"Who is it?" she said, looking Barbara up and down.

"It's me, Balba, your daughter Tanya's friend."

"What brings you here?" And then she realized—"You've
come home. Tanya's been gone a long time. Five years now . . ."

When the store opened, Barbara bought bread, tea, and
sugar with the money that Sogdekon had given her, then went
off with Auntie Darya, returning to Valentina's toward evening
and going to bed right away. The children pestered her with
questions, but Valentina sent them away from her guest. Barbara tried to sleep, but thoughts of her friend Tanya kept her
awake.

Tanya had been born in Irokan, but there was no school
there, so they both had lived at a boarding school. Both were
good, hard-working students. Tanya was especially good at
math. She could count well, and there were no errors in her
notebook. She missed her parents and her native Irokan greatly
and talked about it endlessly. The most beautiful place in the
world for her was the little Irokan River, so wonderful and blue
among the local hills. The sweetest blueberries in the world
grew along the banks of the Irokan. And Tanya would always
say, "The blueberries at Irokan are different. They're unusually
elongated, whereas elsewhere they're round. It makes them
sweeter."

She said that even the *chipiche*—the bluebirds—sang more
sweetly there.

"What do the birds in Bomnak say when they sing?" she once asked Barbara.

"What do you mean?" Barbara answered. "They just chirp."

"Oh no," Tanya smiled. "When birds sing, they always say something. In their own bird language. Perhaps they speak Evenk."

"They just chirp," Barbara said. "They're not people!"

"But they are, they are," Tanya insisted. "And they speak Evenk. Let's go listen someday."

One day she made Barbara get up early and go to the forest, to listen to the birds. It was May, and a bit cold in the early morning. The sun hadn't risen and they went out behind the boarding school, along the bank of the river. Tanya had brought a candle from somewhere.

"What's the *chuvechi* for?" Barbara asked.

"We'll light it, and then you'll hear what the bird says."

"But it'll be light soon enough. Why the candle?"

They sat under the bushes and lit the candle and waited for the birds to wake up. Suddenly, right overhead, Barbara heard it: "*Chiu-chiu, chi-chi!*" the bird sang. "*Ni chuvechi?*"

Barbara started, amazed. Had the bird asked so clearly, "*Chiu-chiu, chi-chi.* Whose candle?"

Tanya elbowed her silently, looking at the candle. "See? She's asking about our candle."

The bird was silent, then asked again, "*Chivi, chi-cha, ni bicha?*"

Barbara's mouth fell open. She clearly understood what the bird was asking. She nearly repeated it aloud—"*Chivi, chi-cha.* Who lived here?" But she held her tongue, covering her mouth with her hand.

"*Chivi, chi-cha, ni bicha?*" the bird asked again and then answered its own question: "*Chuvecki bicha.*"

Now it was Barbara who elbowed Tanya, for she knew that an Evenk by the name of Chuveki had once lived in that part of the woods. And the bird said, "Chuvecki lived here." That was true. He had once lived there.

"*Chiu-chiu, chiu chu,*" the bird sang again. "*Chuveki bicha, chiu chi-cha,*" it then added: Chuvecki is dead. And that was true, too. Barbara knew that Chuvecki had died. But she was amazed at what the bird said next.

"*Chiu-cha, ni chepeche?*"

Puzzled, Barbara looked at Tanya. Who could have drowned? For the bird had asked who had drowned. The bird repeated the question again and again.

"*Chiu-cha, chiu-cha!*" the bird chirped. "*Ni chepecha? Ni chepecha?*" Then it flew away.

"What's that got to do with us?" Barbara said. "*Chiu-cha, chiu-cha!*" she repeated. "Who drowned? Who drowned?" She got up to go.

Then she thought she heard the question again—Who drowned? Who drowned?—and she knew there must be a reason why the bird had asked.

Later, when Irokan shut down, Tanya and her parents had moved to Bomnak. Then she lived at home, while her mother— Auntie Darya—scrubbed floors at the club, and her father hunted. Whenever her father would come home, they ate many wonderful delicacies from the taiga forest. Then, like all of the hunters, after two days of drinking, her father would return to the taiga for an entire year. Sometimes Auntie Darya went with him, but Tanya had to stay at home.

Then her father died and Auntie Darya had started drinking, little by little. When Barbara and Tanya finished school, they went off to continue their education. Tanya enrolled at college in Birobijan, to be trained as a librarian. And her mother, left alone, began to drink even more. Since she couldn't read or write, Tanya had to write to the neighbors to inquire about her. And when she realized that her mother was on the verge of a breakdown, she quit school and returned home. She was afraid her mother would fall and die, frozen in the snow, for who would take care of her? Who would pick her up?

Tanya's life hadn't turned out well. She'd been so clever at school, but she had to scrub floors like her mother. Her dreams never came true. Life had become hard, boring, dull. And so she'd started drinking, too. She had a baby—a son—with a newcomer geologist, and it was even more difficult to care for the three of them on a janitor's pay.

As the years passed, she drank more and more. It was easier that way. She found herself a lover among the gold miners. When he came to town with money, he drank excessively and bought drinks for the others. Once, in the fall, when his team had finished work, he brought his friends with him. They drank all week, first at Tanya's home, then on a motorboat several kilometers from the village. A fight broke out. One of the miners was killed and his body was hidden. The miners threatened her to keep her quiet. Tanya did, for she was afraid of her lover. But he didn't trust her. Before long, they went on another boat trip to drink, and it was then that Tanya drowned.

(

Barbara waited for Yegor to come from the taiga. But it was hard for him to get away. It was too far, and he couldn't leave the deer for long. A month passed, and it became awkward for Barbara to stay as a guest at Valentina's. She decided to go to Verhnezeysk, in Baikal-Amur, to look for a job. But there was no regular transportation between Bomnak and Verhnezeysk. The sea was littered with timber. Whole islands of trees—dead in the water—floated on the surface. People went at their risk, only when they couldn't avoid it.

Barbara spent an entire day sitting on the shore, trying to get to Verhnezeysk. Several boats passed by, but there were only men on them. Besides, they were drunk. The following day, Valentina said that Moskalyan was coming back. In order to avoid him, Barbara sat on the shore again, hoping to leave. Finally, she got lucky. After lunch, a boat came from Verhnezeysk, and the owner agreed to take her with him.

"Who are you going to visit?" he asked.

"Nadya Sologon."

"The one who works at our warehouse? I know her. But maybe you shouldn't go. It's windy today. The waves are high. I only have one lifejacket. Shouldn't you stay here? Or is it urgent?"

"Very urgent," Barbara said, remembering Moskalyan. "I'll go. Yes, I'll go."

"Let's hope nothing goes wrong." The man started the motor.

Suddenly, Barbara fished in her pockets, took out some coins, and tossed them into the water, saying to herself, "Let everything go well, River Zeya. Don't treat me like an alien. Help me. This is my *hulgannia*—my gift—for you!"

But on the way the motor broke down. The man fiddled with it for a long time, until the light of day faded and it began to grow dark. They were far out at sea, where the mouth of the river lost itself among the deep waters, out of sight of land.

It was dark by the time the motor was repaired, and so they turned back. Then they struck some drifting timber, capsized, and Barbara went under. And the last thought that ever flashed through her mind was this: "Oh River Zeya, I didn't forget your *hulganni*. Why are you angry with me? Oh my goodness! I'm not drowning in the river, but in the sea. The River Zeya's not to blame . . ."

Gennady Dyachkov (YUKAGIR)
(

Gennady Dyachkov (1945–1983) was born among the Yukagir (Odul) people of Siberia. The Yukagirs, who number fewer than twelve thousand, are considered to be among the oldest ethnic natives of East Siberia. Their traditional economy was based on hunting wild deer and moose, catching fish, and trapping small fur-bearing animals.

Dyachkov served for four years in the Russian Navy on the Pacific, then studied at Moscow State University, graduating with a degree in humanities. He later lived and worked in the Siberian village of Nelemnoye of the Upper Kolyma region, in the Yakut Autonomous Republic now known as Sakha. During his brief literary career he was recognized as a gifted playwright and authored several noted plays, among them *The Red Seagull* and *The Hunter's Son*. He also wrote several short stories, including "Kasbek," an autobiographical tale. He wrote in Russian.

His writings reflect a tragic mood that foreshadows his premature death. During a visit to his sister's apartment in Moscow in 1983, Dyachkov fell asleep, never to wake. A book of his collected writings, including "Kasbek" and three short stories, was published a year after his death.

THE HUNTER'S SON: A ONE-ACT PLAY

THE HUNTER
He is sixty years of age, dressed in animal skins of the taiga forest.

THE HUNTER'S SON
He is thirty-five years of age, dressed in modern denim.

THE BOY
The HUNTER'S grandson, age twelve, dressed like his grandfather.

SCENE
A riverbank in Siberia, near the taiga forest. A teakettle and pot hang over the fire, stage center. Dishes sit on an empty crate that serves as a table. To the rear is a tent. THE HUNTER *and* THE HUNTER'S SON *sit by the fire, each plucking feathers from a wild duck. There is a small radio nearby, and pieces of wood on the ground.*

TIME
Summer. The present.

THE HUNTER'S SON: (*putting the duck aside*) No, father, I can't do it. The down sticks to the skin and the meat.
THE HUNTER: Don't pull gently, just rip it off.
THE HUNTER'S SON: (*lighting a cigarette*) It doesn't matter. I can't do it. I never could. Remember?
THE HUNTER: So, one more week and off you go again. And for how long, this time?

THE HUNTER'S SON: Only three years. You know that. It's my job.

THE HUNTER: Couldn't you stay home for a year? You promised. We'll go hunting. You can help me. I'm old and will die soon. You're my only son. What good are my daughters?

THE HUNTER'S SON: We've discussed this so many times! You must understand. I'm a radio engineer. I work at a factory. If I stay here, I'll lose my job. What can I do here? Learn to hunt? Besides, my wife would never live here.

THE HUNTER: You and your generation! Can't even clean a duck! I shoot a dozen wild ducks and they're all wasted. Your sisters can't dress them, either. They can't smoke fish. When your mother was alive, she could do anything.

THE HUNTER'S SON: Yes, Mother knew how to do everything.

THE HUNTER: Do you remember how many chickens we kept? And now we have none. Your sisters can't even mend the *torbasa,* our own native boots!

THE HUNTER'S SON: What do you want, Father? They have a profession. They're teachers!

THE HUNTER: And what can they teach, if they can't clean a duck or mend boots?

THE HUNTER'S SON: They know everything about their own profession.

THE HUNTER: (*looking at the river*) Look how Nicholas handles that canoe! He can do anything, and he's only twelve. I'll teach him everything he needs to know.

THE HUNTER'S SON: He's quite a boy. To this day I can't paddle a canoe.

THE HUNTER: I feared too much for you. You were a sickly child, my only son. So I taught you nothing. Never took you hunting. And yet I should have taught you. Like with the deer—if you don't teach them how to pull the sledge, they won't do it. Ever!

THE HUNTER'S SON: (*annoyed*) But I've learned to do other things. My *job* is my sledge. I love what I do.

THE BOY: (*entering with a fish in his hands*) Grandpa! Uncle! Look what I caught in the net!

THE HUNTER: What a trout! Now take your knife and skin it. Toss the entrails to the gulls. The rest goes into the pot.

THE BOY: But I want to play now, Grandpa.

THE HUNTER: You can play later. Get to work! When you're in the taiga, you must work.

THE BOY: (*disappointed*) All right. Where's my knife?

THE HUNTER'S SON: Here, I've got it. (*He hands him the knife and* THE BOY *exits with the fish.*) Why'd you make him a hunting knife, Father? He'll hurt himself, or someone else.

THE HUNTER: It's all right. Let him practice. I'm preparing my successor. Let him become a hunter like me. I lost my chance with you.

THE HUNTER'S SON: It's not right. He must go on learning. He needs an education.

THE HUNTER: To know the woods, the animals, the birds—is education, too! (THE HUNTER'S SON *turns on the radio to contemporary music.*) What kind of music is that? Shouting, screaming, hollering—it's like a bunch of drunks fighting.

THE HUNTER'S SON: It's the latest rock group. Do you like the beat?

THE HUNTER: What are they beating?

THE HUNTER'S SON: They're not beating anything. They're making music . . . to that beat.

THE HUNTER: The devil! I can't stand classical music either. They hold that piece of wood to the throat—what's it called?—a violin. And the noise violates your ears. But I do like that one Frenchman on the radio. He has a good orchestra. He can really play!

THE HUNTER'S SON: Paul Moria?

THE HUNTER: That's him. I used to lie down in the tent and search the airwaves for him, and when I found him, I got the feeling I wasn't alone in the forest. There's everything in that music—the glitter of snow, the murmur of the river, the rustle of the trees. It's like your soul singing.

THE HUNTER'S SON: You're talking about loneliness again, Father. But everyone's soul is lonely.

THE HUNTER: No, son. Your mother and I lived as one soul.

THE HUNTER'S SON: (*turning off the radio*) Then why did you torment her with your drinking?

THE HUNTER: And who doesn't drink nowadays? I didn't drink often, just when I wasn't in the taiga. The forest always cures me. (*A distant splash is heard.*) Did you hear that? Do you know what that is?

THE HUNTER'S SON: How should I know? Just some noise . . .

THE HUNTER: It's the fish playing. Breaking the surface. You have to hear and know every sound in the taiga. It's a science.

THE HUNTER'S SON: (*reluctantly*) Perhaps.

THE HUNTER: Please stay for a year. I'll teach you everything. How to catch muskrat, sable . . .

THE HUNTER'S SON: It's too late for that. I've learned other things.

THE HUNTER: (*with reproach*) You don't like your native land.

THE HUNTER'S SON: (*annoyed*) Here we go again! I love my native land! I often dream of the riverbank. I see Mother and you standing there. But a man needs a job that he likes, and friends with common interests.

THE HUNTER: (*picking up a piece of wood*) So I've cut this birch root for nothing.

THE HUNTER'S SON: (*puzzled*) What's a birch root got to do with it?

THE HUNTER: From the birch root you can make a good handle for a hunting knife. It won't crack in a lifetime. I meant it for you . . .

THE HUNTER'S SON: Why would I need a hunting knife in town? You need special permission to carry one. Better get me some furs instead.

THE HUNTER: (*with a sigh*) I've tried, but you can't get them now. It's easier in winter. What do you want them for, anyway?

THE HUNTER'S SON: A friend asked me to get him one. And what about a bearskin rug? It's so exotic!

THE HUNTER: All that is just whim. Fashion. Look at me. I've taken so many different game animals in my life, yet I still go about in this old deerskin jacket. And my hat is plain. (*He reaches for the kettle.*)

THE HUNTER'S SON: As they say, a shoemaker never wears his own shoes. (*He jumps up.*) Please sit. I'll pour the tea. (*He pours tea into mugs.*)

THE HUNTER: You care for me like a child.

THE HUNTER'S SON: I'm just paying my dues.

THE HUNTER: Don't pay them to me, but to your ancestors— your grandmother and grandfather. You owe your dues to the hunting tradition.

THE HUNTER'S SON: It's too late, Father. It's too late. (*They drink tea.*)

THE HUNTER: Well, I've lost you, all right.

THE HUNTER'S SON: Do you remember Victor, Father?

THE HUNTER: Motya's son? Of course. He drowned last summer. His corpse came to the surface on the sixth day, all by itself. They say he was drunk.

THE HUNTER'S SON: He graduated from aviation school but stayed in the village as a tractor mechanic—because of his parents.

THE HUNTER: And so?

THE HUNTER'S SON: We were friends. Right before his death I got a letter from him. Do you think he drowned by accident?

THE HUNTER: Of course. The boat capsized. That's all.

THE HUNTER'S SON: I'm not so sure. He complained in his letters that he didn't like working as a tractor mechanic. He said he'd go away . . .

THE HUNTER: People say all sorts of things. He capsized at full speed, making a sharp turn. His head struck the boat. He was wounded, unable to swim . . . (THE BOY *runs in with a kettle.*)

THE BOY: Grandpa! I've done everything! (*He holds out the cleaned fish.*)

THE HUNTER: Let me see. Good job! Just like a real woodsman! Put it in the pot.

THE BOY: (*dropping the fish into the pot over the fire*) Grandpa! Uncle! Make me a bow! I'll shoot at crows. I won't shoot the gulls—they're good. How they fought just now over the entrails of that fish!

THE HUNTER: Ask your uncle. He'll make you a good bow.

THE HUNTER'S SON: What? Why does he need a bow? In the village he'll shoot someone by accident.

THE HUNTER: Never mind. I'll make you one later. You'd better sit down now and clean one of these ducks. See, your uncle hasn't finished.

THE BOY: (*regretfully*) I want to play, Grandpa.

THE HUNTER: Sit down. Sit down. You're going to clean this duck for your mother, and then you'll know how to do it.

THE BOY: For my mother? All right. (*He sits and starts pulling feathers.*) Will they come, Grandpa?

THE HUNTER'S SON: (*puzzled*) Who?

THE HUNTER: (*to his grandson*) They must. Just keep listening. (*to his son*) The she-moose and her young one come to the river this time of day to drink and play.

THE BOY: (*excited*) The baby's so funny—he snorts and stomps. And he gets angry when I call him.

THE HUNTER'S SON: (*curious*) Which fur is better in summer—from a young one or an adult?

THE HUNTER: From the young. It's softer. It won't lose its lacy hair.

THE BOY: (*jumping to his feet*) Grandpa, they're coming! Do you hear the mother trampling the brush?

THE HUNTER'S SON: (*jumping to his feet*) Where? Where are they? I can't see them!

THE HUNTER: They're still in the forest. They'll appear in a minute on the other bank, by that crooked birch.

(THE HUNTER'S SON *slips into the tent and returns with a carbine.* THE HUNTER *and* THE BOY, *intent on the opposite bank, don't notice him.*)

THE BOY: There they are! What a long face that mother has! So ver-r-ry long! And here comes the little one!

THE HUNTER: (*to his grandson*) Well, you will grow up, and that young moose will grow up, and one day he'll be your game. I know where they like to go in the taiga.

THE BOY: (*shouting*) Little moose! Little moose! Swim to us! (*A shot resounds from the carbine.*) Oh, grandpa! He's hit!

(THE HUNTER *and* THE BOY *turn to* THE HUNTER'S SON.)

THE HUNTER'S SON: (*with false modesty*) So. I can do some things, after all. The meat is yours, the fur is mine.

THE BOY: (*in anguish*) He's in pain, Grandpa! He's dying!

THE HUNTER: (*in anger*) Why did you kill that little one? How could you raise a hand to him?

THE HUNTER'S SON: I wanted to prove that I can hunt, too.

THE HUNTER: You're no hunter, you're a poacher! Poachers have no hearts, just big bellies. They spit at the future. They devastate everything. A hunter doesn't just kill—he loves the beasts and birds. He cares . . .

THE BOY: (*crying*) He's not stirring. He's dead! He died, Grandpa! Is that really his mother? She's run away! That can't be his mother!

THE HUNTER: (*to his son*) From now on you're a stranger to us. You can go any time, even tomorrow. And don't come for my funeral.

THE HUNTER'S SON: (*embarrassed*) Father! Wait a minute! Please wait! I . . .

THE HUNTER: Don't call me *father* anymore. You're a stranger. Go! But first, since you shot that little moose, take a knife and dress out its carcass.

THE HUNTER'S SON: But I don't know how!

THE HUNTER: Killing is easy. Now go dress your kill. Don't spoil the hide. Remove the entrails and trim the meat, and bring it here in the canoe.

THE HUNTER'S SON: But I can't handle a canoe! Let me take the boat.

THE HUNTER: Go! And don't touch the motorboat! Any fool can cross a river in that!

THE HUNTER'S SON: This is ridiculous, Father! You never taught me these skills, and now you demand them of me!

THE HUNTER: I never taught you to hunt, but I didn't teach you to kill children, either. Get going!

THE HUNTER'S SON: Ah, well . . . I'll go. (*He starts off, then returns.*) Forgive me, Father! Let me stay for six months. I'll arrange it at work. I'll hunt with you and learn how to do everything. Father, forgive me!

THE HUNTER: Don't beg *my* forgiveness. Ask your nephew instead. It's his game you've stolen.

THE HUNTER'S SON: Forgive me, little Nicholas. (*He takes the knife from* THE BOY.)

THE BOY: Grandpa, I'll go with my uncle and help him.

THE HUNTER: No! Let him do everything himself.

(THE HUNTER'S SON *exits.*)

THE BOY: But he can't paddle a canoe.

THE HUNTER: Let him learn. Puppies can't swim either, yet we put them by the collar into the water.

THE BOY: What if he capsizes?

THE HUNTER: He'll swim. He swims well. I've been capsized so many times—just hold the canoe with your hand and swim for shore.

THE BOY: Oh, no! Grandpa, look! He's turned over!

THE HUNTER: Don't panic. Let him swim out by himself. Hang on to the canoe! The canoe!

THE BOY: He's lost it!

THE HUNTER: (*alarmed*) Why doesn't he swim? He's just thrashing about!

THE BOY: He's got the knife in his hand!

THE HUNTER: He's diving! What for? Swim away, Son! Forgive me!

THE BOY: There he is! He's surfaced!

THE HUNTER: What's the matter with him? He's diving again! Son!

THE BOY: The nets are in there, Grandpa! He's caught in the nets! He's trying to cut himself free!

THE HUNTER: He's stubborn, that one! And he's keeping silent, too! Quickly! The boat! Let's go help him! (*They exit stage right.*)

Curtain.

VLADIMIR SANGI (NIVKH)

(

Vladimir Sangi, born in 1935, is a Nivkh writer, folklorist, and political activist from the Pacific Coast region near Sakhalin Island, where his ancestors have lived for centuries. He was born in the Nabil camp, on the east coast of Sakhalin Island and grew up during World War II. Of his early years he says, "From my childhood I remember two things: hunger and folktales." His mother and grandmother told the children stories to dull the pangs of their hunger. By the age of eight Sangi was hunting in order to support his family, but all of the elders had gone to war and there was no one to teach him the traditional skills. The short story included here, "My First Shot," describes his first hunting experience.

In 1959, Sangi graduated from the Herzen Literary Institute in Leningrad (now St. Petersburg). At that time he had already begun the process of recording the ancient traditions of his people, including the lore of the Bear Feast. His first book of prose, *The Nivkh Legends,* was published in 1961 at Yuzhnosakhalinsk. Later, he went for further training in Moscow, in an advanced literary program, where he became the first Nivkh writer to produce a novel, *False Pursuit* (1965). He also contributed to the creation of the Nivkh alphabet and an accompanying textbook for the Nivkh schools. During his Ph.D. studies at the Gorky Institute of World Literature in Moscow, Sangi embarked on his first folklore

expedition (1974). He recorded a Nivkh storyteller at Negliki recit-
ing an epic called "Ikh Myth," which he later remade into the epic
blank verse poem "Song of the Nivkhs." His life since then, however, has been a struggle between high politics, ambitious social/
cultural projects, and writing fiction and poetry. Because of this
divided focus, the quality of his written work has been uneven.

His main books are *False Pursuit, Ikh Myth Legends* (1967),
The Marriage of the Kevongs (1975), which has been translated
into several languages and is considered his best, *A Journey to
Lunvo Camp* (1985), and *The Song of the Nivkh People* (1989).
From 1990–1993, Sangi was president of the Association of Na-
tive Small Nations of North Siberia and the Far East (later called
Raipon) of the Russian Federation.

MY FIRST SHOT

It was very long ago, but I will remember that day forever. I had just turned eight. I remember the date not because my birthday was celebrated in any special way. In my childhood the Nivkh people didn't celebrate birthdays. That was a custom my kinsmen adopted from the Russians much later. All other holidays passed unnoticed as well, without the traditional brightness and joy, because all the men were gone from our village. Only the weak old men and women remained. For a long time the hearts of the elders hadn't stirred to the splash of an oar; for a long time the dugouts with their many oars hadn't disturbed the evening quiet of the bay. Even the gulls had left.

It was a time of hunger. I remember the days when we had but one smoked fish to divide between my brother and me. I thought of him as a grown man in those days, although he was only six years older.

I don't remember my father very well. But I do remember my mother—in the days of plenty—crooked with rheumatism, disregarding it, hobbling on a stick. Eagerly she would go out to the cold shore of the bay to cut up the huge bodies of seals. The long, thin, curved knives went to and fro easily in her weak hands. I was happy, because she had taken me to help. While she sliced open the belly of a seal, I held the edges of its skin thick with fat.

The skin was difficult to hold. My hands tired easily, and the skin would slip from my fingers. Mother scolded me, but I didn't feel bad, because there was plenty to eat in those days.

After my mother had removed the fat from the seal's neck, breast, and stomach, my brother would come over with a sharp knife that Grandpa Lyamzin had made by attaching a Japanese file to a bone handle. Stepping over the mighty neck of the seal, he would plunge his knife into the animal's chest, pressing with all his might. Then the breast would crack apart, baring the ribs. To bare them thus one had to be very strong. And my brother was good at it.

He would cut the seal into many pieces—with finger holes in each, to make them easy to carry—and I would lug the meat to a storage barn that looked just like those chicken coops on stilts in Russian fairy tales. The fat he cut into huge chunks he carried all by himself.

Then we three men—my father, my brother, and I—would sit down at the *pirsh,* a low table, crossing our legs in oriental fashion, and mother would distribute the warm liver. We would cut it into small pieces with our knives, dip it in salt, and eat unhurriedly. But I would swallow noisily, to indicate that the hunter's catch was delicious and I was happy to be fed. Mother and sister sat at another *pirsh,* dipping their fingers into the open skull of the seal, removing the tender brain. To my sister's great joy, the seal's head was as big as a bucket.

My brother would accompany my father on the spring hunt in a dugout. Like all the Nivkh, he was an expert with the craft, which was unsteady and round as a log. He never capsized. Handling the dugout at sea was an art mastered only by the true hunters.

My father and brother used to kill many seals. Nobody would ask who had taken the most. It wasn't polite to ask the name of the benefactor when there were two or more participants in a hunt. What counted was that the people ate their fill.

One day, when the snow had melted and the winds and current had drawn the ice into the sea, my father went away. I was busy chasing chipmunks in the hills. Gone, too, were the fathers of my friends of the same age. Later we understood that they had gone to war.

Before that, we played "hunters and deer." The deer party

had to learn to hide, while the hunters had to find their hiding place and approach noiselessly and unobserved. After my father left, we played war games, dividing into two parties.

My brother and the Russian boy Slava were the commanders. Slava had transparent eyes that looked like glass. I wanted to touch them—to see if they were real.

One of the parties hid in the bushes, while the other advanced. And whenever somebody from the opposite side passed my hiding place, I pointed with a crooked stick that looked like my grandfather's pipe and shot at him.

"Pow!"

If the adversary didn't hear, I shot louder, many times.

"Pow! Pow! Pow!"

Often our entire group charged. Then Slava, like a real commander in the cinema, would leap up and cry, "Follow me! Hurray!" His army would come to meet ours, and I would shoot my stick. It was magic—both pistol and machine gun, whichever I wanted.

I shot at Slava, for it was always an honor to kill a commander. But he didn't fall. And then the hand-to-hand combat started, which we loved. When the enemy fired at you with a machine gun, you had to fall down. If they fired at you with a pistol, you could argue that you were only wounded, or that they had missed you altogether. But no matter how I shot at Slava, he refused to go down. He would chase me and catch me with his strong hands and throw me to the ground. And when I started to complain, he was contemptuous.

"Don't whine! You're the Germans and we're the good guys. We must win!" Then, waving his hand, he would say, "Let's begin again!"

And so we started all over. But this time we were the good guys and Slava's party were the Germans. Yet it was still the same—Slava didn't want to lose.

"You weaklings!" he would shout. "Don't you know that our forces are retreating? Agh!" He was disdainful. "How would you know? You babies!"

Then we would go back to playing hunters and deer.

But somehow we began to meet less often. We had to help our mothers at home. Every day I had to fetch firewood. I always took my magic stick with me, but now it was a rifle for hunting.

Sometimes I played hunter even in our yard, hunting the cans, which were wild ducks. Time passed, and before long, we became accustomed to hunger in our house. It was an everyday thing, as certain as day and night.

My brother, who turned fourteen that summer, joined the team of fishermen. But our family rarely saw any fish. It all went to the war effort, even the small fish and the junk fish—the lean bullheads and sea ruffs.

My brother would come home tired and wet, and I felt ashamed when I saw how exhausted he was from the heavy work.

Grandpa Lyamzin, the elder of our clan, was ancient and weak, but he soon taught me how to fish, and sometimes I brought home a small catch.

Grandpa would sit all day long on the slope of a sandy hill, staring sharply into his binoculars, scanning the sea. Maybe he was waiting to discover among the raging waves the dark spot of a motorboat bringing my father back from war. But my father didn't come, and Grandpa spent his days on the beach, endlessly watching the waves.

My brother was exhausted, yet I couldn't help him in any way.

When the days of hunger came, I caught myself looking now and again at my father's rifle on the wall, hanging from huge deer antlers. It could be of help, but there wasn't anyone to use it. The only provider in our family—my brother—spent all of his time among the fishermen.

I stared at the rifle, full of hope, thinking of the delicious liver, the baked tender fins and tails of seals; of the thick soups of ducks and geese; of deer meat; and even the heart of a bear that my father once had shot in the taiga. That heart had been given to me so that the mighty spirit of the taiga forest and mountains would take away my fears, so that I might grow up strong and become a stalwart provider.

To shoot a real gun was a dream of all Nivkh boys. Many times I asked my brother to let me shoot at some target, so that just for one moment I'd feel like a man. But he wouldn't let me. Ammunition was scarce, and I was too small. But the day I turned eight, he gave me permission.

"Haksun," he said, "here are two cartridges. Go practice on the sandpipers. Press the butt of the rifle tight to your shoulder. It will kick hard."

Slava was sitting with us at the time, and he looked at me somewhat strangely. Nobody had ever looked at me that way before. His pensive look went right through me and continued on, far, far away. In his eyes the fire of amazement blazed coldly for a long time, the way eyes do when regarding something great and unfathomable.

In the hall by the doorway I saw my crooked stick—my machine gun, pistol, and hunting rifle. I almost kicked it aside, but thought better of it, inserting it into a hole between two planks of the wall. It could prove useful someday.

It was a pity to waste cartridges on the sandpipers—small birds that swarmed in huge flocks by the shore. So I went toward the bog, hoping to find some wild ducks. And as I came to a thicket on the crest of a hill, I saw two ducks floating on a little pond in the bog below.

Nivkh children my age knew almost all species of ducks. Those on that pond—by their small size, thin heads, beaks, dark speckled plumage, and hasty movement—I recognized as teals. They were feeding, floating with their heads in the water, their tails above. I could hear their rapid smacking, like the sound of a tiny rivulet, as they passed water through their beaks, gleaning small insects and other creatures. From time to time they raised their heads, watching for danger.

This was my first hunt. No one had taught me the skills. My brother was away, Grandpa Lyamzin had stopped hunting years ago, and all the rest had gone to war. I don't know where my hunting ability came from. From my blood, I guess—inherited.

It was too far from the thicket at the crest of the hill to the ducks below. I had to get closer, unobserved. I had to go down an open slope and crawl to an overgrown hummock. Or I could make a long detour around the bog and approach from the opposite bank. But I discarded that possibility. I was afraid to lose time. The ducks might fly off. I didn't know then that ducks wouldn't leave a bog that's rich in food without good cause.

I had to get closer, right out in the open, a risky move. My clothes—both shirt and trousers—were barely visible against the sandy terrain. This helped me make a decision. Just as the two ducks lowered their heads into the water, I left the thicket on the hill and, watching them closely, took several quick steps, my bare feet noiseless on the damp and sandy ground.

One of the ducks raised her head, and I instantly froze in an awkward position, arm and rifle outstretched. I even stopped blinking.

Would she notice?

The duck turned her head and looked at me closely, getting ready to take off. The other, even if it didn't see me, would do the same, trailing drops of water behind.

That duck must have seen me, a strange object. But she looked confused because that strange object was standing so still. Maybe she was thinking that it had been there all along, only she hadn't noticed.

The duck began eating again, and the other, having stopped for a moment too, did the same. I quickly advanced down the hill, and when the ducks raised their heads again, I was sitting behind the cover of a sparse thicket, ten paces from a hummock overgrown with *ledum,* a wild tea of the marsh. I had to get to that hummock, but it was too low. Even if I crouched, I couldn't get close. The ducks would notice. There was only one way—by crawling.

The thought that I was hunting suddenly captivated me completely. This was my first hunt! I wanted to return with my kill!

Without hesitation I lay down in the icy water of the bog. Its chill numbed my body and took my breath away. My clothes stuck to my skin, hindering my movements, but I crawled forward, keeping the rifle high so it wouldn't get wet.

Then I reached the hummock, the ducks just twenty feet away. They were quiet, continuing to eat. I braced my rifle securely on the hummock and took another breath. The ducks were sitting very low in the water, with only their backs above the surface. It would be difficult to hit them. I decided to wait for them to merge into one, to get them both with one shot, but they never did. So I aimed at the nearest one and squeezed the trigger. Although I held the butt tight against my shoulder, it kicked back at me sharply. But I didn't feel the pain.

Frantically the ducks took flight. One went low to the side, the other rising straight up, its head strangely askew, and I knew that it was wounded. It froze for a second, suspended in midair, then spread its wings and fell somewhere on the opposite shore. The other flew to her mate, crying in excitement.

Holding tight to my rifle, knee deep in mud, I ran through the bog toward the opposite shore. The wounded bird was missing, its mate crying loudly, curving her tail queerly in distress.

My first reaction was to shoot at her, but I was afraid to frighten the other, which was already wounded. What if I missed! I would come home empty-handed.

I looked for the wounded duck a long time, its mate getting in my way at every step. I felt pity for her.

After some time, however, her cries ceased. By that time I felt guilty I hadn't killed the other outright—it was so close that I wouldn't have missed.

I continued to look, and suddenly—between the branches of a thicket—I saw my duck. The sun was shining on its smooth belly. Filled with joy, I grabbed it and ran home, leaving the other for another day.

(

Mother took out coupons for flour from her thin wallet. Whenever we could, we saved these coupons until the end of the month to buy our flour all at once, so at least once a month we could feel that we had eaten enough.

But that day, although it was nowhere near the end of the month, my mother took the coupons and bought some flour.

Then the old women and Grandpa Lyamzin gathered at our house to share the meal. They ate heartily, licked the bones of my game, and praised the hunter.

After supper, while the old women were taking turns smoking the same pipe, Grandpa Lyamzin came up to me, tenderly put his big hand on my thin shoulders, looked carefully into my eyes, and said in a voice that had grown unexpectedly quiet, "I knew you would become a real man."

Then he looked aside, blinked, and added with apparent sadness. "But I didn't think you'd become one so early."

Maria Vagatova (KHANTY)

(

A Native Siberian of the Khanty people, **Maria Vagatova** is a poet and storyteller. The oldest of twelve children in the family of a reindeer breeder, she was born in 1936 in a taiga forest village near the Kazym River, a tributary of the Ob, and spoke only Khanty until the age of seven. She called her grandfather her first teacher of literature and later took his family name as her nom de plume.

Following her graduation from the Khanty-Mansiisk Pedagogical Institute in 1965, Vagatova organized and led a Native folksong group while working as a teacher. The Khanty poet Vladimir Voldin urged her to publish her poetry. After their marriage, Voldin suddenly disappeared during a business trip and was later found hanged, leaving Maria to care for their four children. In 1970, Vagatova began writing for a Khanty newspaper, creating folk tales for children, and recording Khanty folklore as told by Native storytellers.

In collaboration with the Khanty poet Andrei Tarkanov, she published *Khanty and Mansi Folktales* (1977). Her first poetry collection, *Morning on the Ob River,* was published in 1987. *Little Tundra Man,* her bilingual (Russian/Khanty) collection of tales and poetry, appeared in Tyumen, Siberia, in 1996, followed in 2003 by *My Song, My Song,* a handsome book of verse and short prose illustrated by the Khanty artist Gennady Raishev.

Maria Vagatova lives in Khanty-Mansiisk. She has seven grandchildren. She writes in Khanty and Russian, taking as her themes the home landscape of the Khanty people, its rivers and forests, and her Native language itself. The following selections are from *Me Ariem, Ariem* (My Song, My Song).

MY WORD, MY TONGUE

If I couldn't hear my own words,
if I didn't know my own language:
who would listen?
How on Earth would I live?
Every branch of the tree of language
is sacred to my people:
the smallest root of my words
binds the threads of their hearts.
If I couldn't hear my own words,
if I didn't know my own language:
who would listen?
How on Earth would I live?

RIVER MOSUM, MY WATER

River Mosum, my water,
I have adorned you with ski trails.
River Mosum, my land,
I have planted you with footpaths.
I have carried on you
heavy loads of red hides,
heavy loads of white hides,
every one!
And now old age has claimed me.
Old age has taken this woman.
The twin barrels of my shotgun
are rusted.
My two-barreled shotgun
is rusty.
The tracks I've left on land and water
are snow covered two fathoms deep.
The paths I've blazed on land and water
are overgrown with thick moss.
Old age has claimed me.
Old age has taken this woman.
May young girls discover
my lost tracks.
May young men discover
my hunting tricks.
Mosum River, my water,
I bequeath to them forever.
Mosum River, my land,
I forever bequeath.

DIRGE FOR THE LAND OF THE KHANTY

My forests, adorned with necklaces
of many-colored beads,
my groves of waving rushes
in rust-colored bogs—
all lie trodden and trampled,
swallowed and devoured
by the greedy mouth of quicksand.
My embroidered rainbow ribbons
of many-colored cloth
lie trampled in black bogs.
Multilayered, many-colored
shades of rainbow hues
have been stomped into black silt.

I hear the wail of Mother Earth:
"They have pulled the hairs from my head
one by one,
they have yanked out many strands
one by one.
The ornaments of my headdress
fall apart.
My rainbow necklaces
have been plucked out by the roots.
My very breath has gone up in smoke."

O generous Father-Light,
I am about to expire!
O great Mother Earth,
How should I live now?
An air of dread infuses my spirit.

My body is covered with cold slime.
My breath has receded deep into my heart.
My tears of grief, my calamitous tears,
have been absorbed by the earth
like the rain itself.
But the tears of my Sacred Mother:
Where shall they go?

THE PEOPLE OF TUK'YAKANG VILLAGE

I make my way to Tuk'yakang Village,
gazing deep into the land
from the seat of my sledge.
Rows of trees, covering high hilltops
like a patterned ribbon, draw nearer.
I gaze deep into the land
where green trees thrive. I grasp them
with my eyes and wonder.
Happiness fills my soul.
My heart embraces lake after lake,
strewn like a necklace,
and wonders.
Rivers and streams run in patterns.
Their circles and arches
are highways
where fish live and travel.
I see them moving along with me.
These are the homes of fish
heavy with caviar.
I find boat trails and sledge paths
of people who have passed this way,
holding them in my heart as I follow
their lead.

In Tuk'yakang Village
I place my feet on the land
of people I have never met before,
Khanty I have never seen,
people who greet me with news of life,
news of beasts and birds and people

near and far. They adorn my heart
with ornaments of beasts and birds alike,
patterned after the creatures
of forests and lakes.
The Khanty of Tuk'yakang Village
have captured my heart.
The people of Tuk'yakang Village
have captured my soul.

STONE SOLDIER

A stone soldier makes his home
in the green forest:
the sun is his fireplace,
the sky is his roof.
Mother Earth has drunk
the hot blood he shed.
The people have hidden his heart
from his enemies.
They were unable to kill him.
Because of him
there is light on this Earth.
Because of this light
he lives in every heart
with warmth and joy.
Because of him
the ice melts every spring.
The lives he has protected
become the fresh floods of spring,
and in the splash of that water
I hear his song:

"You, too, are soldiers.
So live well, like the men you are.
Don't waste your heart's energy,
your breath or blood.
They are needed for the people,
for the Earth itself.
For Man will not die.
The Earth lives in his blood.
Flowers grow, life breathes,

and people walk
the straight wide road.
Though I am now a stone soldier,
I live for the ages,
preserved by my people
in stone."

A stone soldier makes his home
in the green forest:
the sun is his fireplace,
the sky is his roof.
His fiery heart lights the Earth
more than the sun.

AN OLD ANTHILL

That old anthill
looks like a forlorn yurt,
abandoned, its roof
caved in.
No ants remain,
just passageways,
their living nerves
woven round about.
These are their walking paths
overgrown with grass and moss.

I see hunters and fishermen
seeking this yurt,
bringing their people
to hunt and fish in the
forests, lakes, and rivers.
How many needles and twigs
they have gathered!
How often this ant-clan
walked these ways!
How much energy it took
to build this anthill!

I see their ancestors:
what strength they needed
in their arms and legs
to build this vibrant house!
Leaves, pine needles, tree bark—
nobody wants them anymore.
They rot here in vain, useless.

But I can't imagine anything else.
It's as if your closest kin
has departed forever.
An old anthill, a forlorn yurt—
needles, leaves, tree bark—
ancient materials of the Khanty.
I feel pain in my heart.

I see the children's playground.
I hear their laughter and voices
mocked by the forest's echo.
Here is a pine tree:
a rope was fastened
on its thick branch
for a child's swing.
That tree rocked them well.

I see places where the Khanty
crafted the tools of daily life
from wood, roots, and brimstone
with the help of an ax or knife.
I know these sacred places
by their blackened woodchips.
Here they made oars and boats.
Here fish traps were woven.
From tree roots they processed
strong cords to repair their wares.

I see a sledge
about to rush off!
Twenty-six little legs support
its runners—the sledge
for a bride—its twenty-six thin legs
like the legs of a crane.

It runs on ahead.
I can see it!
But they're not made anymore.
They no longer exist.

Old anthill,
why did you catch my eye?
To remind me of the fate of
forlorn yurts?
Is that why you've touched
my heart so deeply?
You were a part of my blood.
I have known much joy,
but my heart isn't happy
due to memories you've stirred:
Forlorn anthill!
The very water of my blood
pours out, drenching the tracks
about this old yurt,
running into the earth.

Gennady Raishev (KHANTY)

(

Gennady Raishev, born in 1933, is the son of a Khanty hunter whose family survived World War II and the famine that followed by hunting.

In 1954, Raishev began his studies at Hertzen University in Leningrad (now St. Petersburg), specializing in literature. After his second year he began classes at the evening art school, ultimately graduating with dual certificates. Although he pursued his art in Surgut, in West Siberia, in the Ural Mountains, and elsewhere, his first important solo exhibition did not occur until 1988, in Sverdlovsk and Tyumen. In the 1990s his gift as an artist received national recognition with many solo shows and a joint exhibition with N. Scott Momaday at the Artists' House in Moscow. Raishev's permanent studio in Khanty-Mansiisk is now a memorial museum open to the public.

During his formative years as an artist, Raishev was influenced by many artistic movements—postimpressionist, surrealist, realist, and classical. But most obvious is the heritage of the Khanty legendary and mythological past. He employs black-and-white techniques mainly in printmaking but also works in oil and watercolor. He has illustrated books by such prominent Khanty figures as Yeremei Aipin and Maria Vagatova, and several books feature his own extensive works.

His style is unique, expressive, and readily recognizable, as the four prints in this collection demonstrate. As he states, "[Art] must be mysterious. The Khanty people love fantasies, and you cannot fantasize within the classic canon. The Native tradition employs flat surfaces, and all is symbolic, which gives the freedom to fantasize. Such freedom demands a new artistic language, which I am well on my way to exploring, as I go forth with a hope and a dream."

GennaDY RaISHeV

(

Forest (1972)

Taiga (1968)

Moose (1968)

Loons (1982)

Jansi Kimonko (UDEGEH)

(

Jansi **Kimonko** (1905–1949) was the first writer to emerge among the Udegeh, a native people numbering about two thousand who live in the woodlands in the Far South of Eastern Siberia, near the Sea of Okhotsk. Their territory is close to the Amur River and the present city of Khabarovsk. Kimonko represents the older generation of emerging authors among the Native Siberian peoples. He was born on the banks of the Sukpai River and spent his childhood hunting in the taiga forest. During the Civil War of 1918–19, he helped the Red Revolutionary forces, working as a guide. Later, in 1928, he was educated in Khabarovsk, then in Leningrad, at the Institute of the Peoples of the North, where his writing career began.

In 1936, Kimonko was arrested on the false charge of espionage and imprisoned for two years. During World War II he served in the Russian Coast Guard in the Russian Far East. Following the war, back home in the Sukpai River region, he became the head of a local hunters' union and began working on an autobiographical novel, *Where the Sukpai Rushes Along,* influenced by his friend, the journalist Julia Shestakova, who meticulously translated the work from Udegeh into Russian.

The first three parts of this novel, published in 1948, were later translated and published in France, Poland, Hungary, and Germany. Kimonko's premature death—he was killed by a bear—

was predicted by an old woman, and his tribesmen believed that one of his enemies had turned into a bear to take revenge on the writer. The novel remains unfinished.

The beginning of the novel follows, relating details of the ancient Udegeh migration and voicing a hymn to the Sukpai River.

From WHERE THE SUKPAI RUSHES ALONG

Oh, Sukpai River—native land of my father and grandfathers! My forefathers discovered you. Following the tracks of the otter, they came to you from the Samarga River. They came to your very headwaters, first ascending magnificent mountains to get through the pass, a pass glistening with rocks, a pass lower than Ulia, the greatest of all Sukpai summits. At the crest, long ago, there was a lake, now but a white crater. You can see the stars on clear days from high on Ulia.

Who knows when it was? The ancient stories are as dim as the light of the morning star.

My ancestors cherished memories of their forefathers for ages and ages as they migrated along the seashore. There were many, and they called themselves the tribe of Kia. And there was a time when Chief Kia was famous for his strength and wisdom. But one day he went to war with another chief, Kukchinka, over the beautiful Alagda. It was a frightening war and Kukchinka won. He killed Kia and scattered his tribe through the mountains and woods.

Who knows how often the rivers changed course, how often the taiga forest changed its clothes, since my ancestors first came to the seashore? Fleeing their enemies, they no longer wanted to be known as the tribe of Kia. They lost many of their brothers on the way, broke many arrows on the rocks. They lit a fire and carried it away with them, shielding it from water and wind. Waters big and small crossed their path. Rivers flowed to the sea, and the sea was deep and mysterious.

For many years my forefathers lived by the Kimo River. At the Time of Big Water a calamity struck—dams were swept away, and fish traps with them. The fish went to the sea. Days of famine followed. And the wisest of our clan said, "Let us go live in the forest!" And in the cedar forest our people found food. They ate nuts and drank water. At every nomad camp they left behind fresh graves under grass mounds. And then the river flashed before them, its banks covered with grasses. Here the *chugunya*—the marsh grass—grew tall, stretching its broad leaves on round fragrant stems. *Luktas* flowered in the quiet creeks, and their roots gave strength to the tired. Everywhere grew thickets of *aunta* with their sweet and juicy little roses. The wondrous grasses led afar. But high mountains stood in the way.

"Shouldn't we climb to the top?" The strangers paused in thought, resting at the foot of the highest mountain before ascending to the pass, where the shaman spoke in incantations. Everyone repeated his words after him, addressing the kind spirits who lend success on the road. And everyone left a personal sign on the mountain—a piece of ragged clothing on a branch, a ribbon of moose hide, a tuft of grass on a pole.

They say that otter tracks led my forefathers to the river itself. And they called it the *Sukpai,* which means ray of the sun.

And having reached the Sukpai, they saw that it flowed into a large river. On the banks of that river were many tracks of wild game. There was much food in the river itself. Beasts came at night to feast in the quiet creeks, striking fish with their hooves. It was no accident that my ancestors made their way through that pass. They called the large river *Huu,* which means the Chorus, a chorus of many rivers. The Kimonko clan was the first to float through it in their dugout canoes. How many poplars there were for making boats! Hunters began going down the rivers, up the rivers.

But my forefathers chose to stay and live on the Sukpai.

And now it glistens before me, the Sukpai! Ascending the mountain, I take my carbine from my shoulder and survey the valley at length, opening my eyes to the *sopkas,* the humped mountains crowded below in white mists. For hundreds of miles around me there are only forests and mountains. Birds listen to the waters talk; rivers listen to the birds sing. Here my grandfather grew up and grew old. Here my childhood ran, weeping and laughing, through the noisy creeks and forest moss.

And so I remember you, Sukpai—native land of my father and grandfathers! Your water rushes and foams at the shoals. Your powerful current carries along great stones, and your rapids are terrible—Oh, Sukpai!

On you flow, churning up rocks from below, turning them over—rocks huge and small, rough and smooth—as if at play. From the mountain crests you make your first drop, then receive your tributaries like brothers—Bolinku, Tugumu—to flow as one large river, never ceasing your work. Land opens where water had been; water appears where land had been. Cutting off promontories, you build shoals and make new banks. Powerful streams become old riverbeds, riverbeds become land, and still you flow on, raising your voice to the woods and mountains.

> Sukpai—the way to Bikin!
> Sukpai—the way to Idzi!
> Sukpai—the way to the ocean!
> There the *kharius* fish lay their eggs,
> the *taimen* fish and *lenki* fish run swift;
> there the moose feeds at quiet creeks,
> bears cross from one side to the other;
> there otters mass at the foot of steep cliffs,
> sables crouch along the banks. . . .
> All this is the Sukpai—my native land!

Anna Nerkagi (TUNDRA NENETS)

(

Born in 1952, **Anna Nerkagi** is a Nenets writer from the Yamal Peninsula in the Far North of West Siberia. After graduating from Tyumen Industrial University, she published her first autobiographical story, "Aniko of the Nogo Clan," in 1977. Then she faced a life crisis. Influenced by the American author Jack London and his writings of the Alaskan North, Nerkagi was torn between her career as a writer and the traditional life of her people.

From Tyumen, Nerkagi returned to the Yamal Peninsula, dividing her time between her writing and the traditional nomadic life of a reindeer owner. She recorded many traditional songs before turning from folklore to political picketing in 1987 in an effort to halt the industrial invasion of the Yamal Peninsula, which, because of its huge natural gas deposits, became the "Russian Klondike" during the 1990s. Nerkagi lives in the Yamal Tundra, at the small village of Laborovaya, educating adopted Nenets children. She has recently joined the Russian Orthodox Church.

Nerkagi's writing includes the short novels *Aniko of the Nogo Clan, Ilir* (1979), *The White Yagel* (1986), and *The Horde* (1992–98). The following excerpt from *The Horde* is dedicated to the "memory of the martyred Daniel Andreev," son of the famous Russian writer Leonid Andreev and godson of Maxim Gorky. A poet and novelist, Andreev was sentenced to twenty-five years in prison in 1947 because his writing did not reflect sanctioned

Soviet reality. Released in 1957 after a review of such cases under Nikita Khrushchev, he died in 1959, his health ruined from a heart attack suffered while incarcerated. The piece is highly symbolic and parabolic in nature. In its opening Nerkagi foresees the details of humanity's apocalypse.

From THE HORDE

In memory of the martyred Daniel Andreev

I am afraid of my own prophecies because my presentiments come true. This requires caution with the Word, especially with the one that comes from the spirit at the peak of elation, like a strange illness. When the mind is hot, the inner vision sees things that go unnoticed in a normal state. Then it is possible to see all, to tell all. The mind captures the tiniest grains of thought, yet I can't remember the gift of sight. I can't remember my eyes at all. It's as if I were blind. No letters, no words, no lines—nothing is seen. Only the pulse of the thought exists, the living breath of that which is written and perceived.

It is terrifying to think that something may guide the mind and soul. That someone may direct the will, clad in words uttered in the throes of illness. This is the only way I can describe the delirium of the spirit that engulfs me time and again.

God forbid, if by this Word I unwittingly sign the death sentence of my small people, whom I love so much. Is it God or the Devil who leads me? I cannot say. If it is God, may His will be fulfilled. But what if it's the Devil? Then I am most afraid—to the very tips of my trembling fingers.

. . . I foresee the final failure ahead. It shall come to all of us. It won't be due to cancer, or AIDS, but some other illness. The Soul has begun to rot inside of us, in the way that any organ in a mortal body can rot: the liver, the lungs, the kidney. . . .

In the killing of the deer I see the beginning of the end for the Nenets people. The Nenets have stopped seeing the deer as their life-brother. They see only another piece of meat to satisfy their hunger or vanity. But hunger is always the forerunner of death.

. . . When you cut down a tree, its sap runs inside for some time. The decaying trunk gives its last efforts to feed the limbs, to give shelter, shrinking with each new day. It dries up slowly, without any sign of agony.

This is the way my people will die. We convince ourselves that we are alive, that we are healthy, that we are prosperous, but like the dying tree we cast a shadow.

This is how it is going to be. . . . I do not say this in malignant joy, but in sadness.

Let me be mistaken. Let my words be but the delirium of a Soul in illness. Let all that is written be but a moment's despair.

(

The old gray Eagle flapped his wings and, borne along by the stroke, searched for a place to die. He wanted a warm, dry, sunny place.

His energy was ebbing. The stroke of his own wings left him powerless, and his eyes, hindered by tears of death, could not find the place he desired. Sharp black cliffs, reflecting the red rays of the sunset, spread away in the distance, but there was no suitable spot in sight.

Irresistibly, the earth pulled him closer. The Eagle raised himself once more on numbed wings and gave a cry of pain and anguish. His cry struck the black cliffs, and it seemed that the cliffs also cried.

The sky could hold him no longer. The air rushed through his feathers and he understood that he was falling, falling like a stone. Then he was down and the sky died above him, and his last thought was: there will be no more sky. He had been the last Master of the Sky, alone for many years, for there were no small birds left. The skies had become empty quite suddenly, and he, weakened and stunned with fear, had rushed from one ridge to another, until exhausted.

For three years, searching for his tribesmen, he had sent

loud calls in vain through the wasted mountains and the sky above them, his throat hot and aching, then finally silent. In the last summer of his life he had flown to visit the old and vacated nests of other eagles, meeting death everywhere—in the devastated nests, in the caves and canyons.

Now it was time to die. To remain alone in the enormous sky would be too lonely. And the Eagle was dead even before he fell. As he wished, his body fell not on the cliffs but into a small crevice in the rocks bedded with silvery moss. The soft grave absorbed his weight, and had he been conscious, he would have been content. The old Eagle was wise. The resting place he had chosen for his head and bones was a high mountain, with three ranges equidistant from each other. Their black hills were a reminder of people ascending, bent by the burden of the way, or perhaps the burden of thought. Close by them, the small rocks were like children. It was as if all of them, frightened by something, had begun to ascend the high mountain in droves, but— never having fulfilled the Great Way—had turned into stone. So where had they gone? To whom?

The very summit of the high mountain contained a place very similar to what had once been called the Playground, a stretch of level terrain with space enough for a great number of people, animals, and children—the most beautiful spot on Earth. Here the people would play. When there was life, the Playground resounded with song for days on end. Then the noises of the people, the beasts, and the birds were silenced, and only one song could be heard, proud, courageous, and wonderful. Everyone—the skies, the stones, the beasts—listened to it. And when it ended, the people talked. Then the Word of humans was heard at the Playground, and again the skies, the stones, and the beasts listened.

The people of the Seven Lands came together at the Playground. They came from afar, and they brought with them their children, girls, old men, the blind, the depraved, the dying. Everyone must play at least once in a lifetime. Woe to him who neglected the Playground! To die without having played was considered shameful.

For seven days the people played. For seven days the people and children laughed, the old men, too, and the women, the depraved, the dying. The animals played also. The sky could not stand still when the humans played. For seven days the sun was happy, looking down on the Playground. The Gods, seen only by a few, would descend to play among the people. The place chosen for the Playground was honored and glorious, a sacred expanse where the people of the Seven Lands frolicked.

After playing, the people would leave what they could afford at the Playground: coins, silver dishes, decorative copper, white gold. Their gifts were a sign that the people had played well; that at the core of their play had been peace; and that in peace would their lives continue. By looking at the Playground you could sense the spirit of any century.

The high mountain with its three ranges, lit by the setting sun, was just this kind of place. Had it once been a Playground? No one knows. Was it a place of sacred worship? That's unknown as well. But at the moment when the last bird fell from the sky—that lonely doomed Eagle—it was already a place of grief, and the dying cries of the bird stirred the eerie silence. For not only the old Eagle had sought rest there. Bones lay scattered as far as the eye could see—skulls, limbs, spines. Some were rooted in the earth and stuck out like trees. Others were rotten, almost disintegrated. Still others shone with tints of pink, crimson, blue, and green. Tiny skeletons of the smallest birds lay by larger skeletons, as if some fierce battle had taken place there, as if the birds and beasts—perhaps people, too— had begun some conflict, which no one survived. Had someone violated the law while playing? Had someone been overcome by evil, killing his neighbor? Had the fire of enmity raged out of control, so that no one could extinguish it? That is why only bones—no coins, silver, copper, or gold, the signs of peace—littered the breast of the Earth. Was Death breathing on the current age of man?

Or was it that, like the Eagle, exhausted by despair, everyone had willingly sought out a place of grief, so future generations could grasp the tragedy of the past? Whatever the reason, the summit of the high mountain, littered with bones, was no Playground. Nor was it a sacred place of worship, like the ones people had once visited, people now lost in the darkness of time.

Cast a glance from the top of that strange mountain and the thought of awesome tragedy returns. The land, spreading all around, carries not the smallest sign of life. Miles away from the three ranges of this high mountain—a mountain that has lost its name—other mountains lie upturned, baring their bowels, shamelessly and mercilessly. The land that lies between them has no grass, just an occasional sprout or stunted tree. And everywhere the endless waters lie stagnant.

(

Far from the Mountain That Lost Its Name, in the interior of the Earth, away from forests large and small, lies the Horde. This is the only way to define that gathering of pale, frightened, forsaken people. They exist like ants in an enormous anthill. But at least in an anthill there is order and law, a division of labor. In the name of labor, each industrious ant brings to the anthill each blade of grass, each grain of sand. But in the Horde . . .

The horrible Horde is like a nest of worms ingesting filth, then feeding on each other. Its origin is painful to relate. The people of the Horde are descendants of those who were once rooted in labor. The essence of their life was the deer—that beautiful animal with four legs, a fluffy tail, and wonderfully warm fur of different colors, from bluish-black to light blue, like the lake's morning mist.

The crowning greatness of the deer was its antlers. They grew on the top of its head like rays of the rising sun, sprouting through the fur and gradually turning to strong bone, then gracefully branching. In a similar way songs are born. The antlers were the deer's song, so the ancestors would say. The deer and the people lived one life, so closely connected that the death of the one became the death of the other, both physically and spiritually.

The people of the Horde survive as best they can. Some inhabit houses with big eyes—the windows—houses as cold as a forest clearing in the dead of winter. Others live in little, half-dark huts bent close to the ground. The oldest of the Horde live in strange conic dwellings that are difficult to describe. They are full of holes, as fragile as paper in a strong wind. The people are pitiful and poor. In winter, like moles, they do not come out at all, and the young members of the Horde mock them, teaching their children to do likewise.

These moles live by themselves, on the worst land, where the earth is a swamp, yet in winter it becomes as hard as asphalt. They often gather in one dwelling and sit close to each other, crouching on the balls of their feet, their gray heads lowered, staring for hours into the fire. Their faces reflect memory and grief. The men rest their hands on sheaths that hang at their sides, the only remnant of the past. And their fingers tremble.

The women sit in torn black dresses on the other side of the fire, guarding the entrance, for enmity is old. Its roots are deep and cannot be traced, because these moles of the Horde were the last free ones. For a long time they did not acknowledge the Horde itself, and it was they who gave the Horde its scornful name—*Khaly-Mya*—the dwelling place of worms. The members of the Horde scorned them in turn, calling them the Dirty Ones.

The dwelling place of worms is the largest in these lands, near the stony belt of the Earth, the weather-beaten polar mountain range of the Urals. Close by trickles the narrow stream with the name of *Shuchja*—the Pike River—a reminder of the time when this terrifying fish plied these waters, now long gone.

The Horde originated in "revolutionary times" of old, a name given to that era when human folly led to the present loss of spirituality, the most terrible of human diseases. The folly was deep, no way out could be discovered, and the people lay entangled like mosquitoes in a spider's web.

This particular Horde, in the beginning, was an ethnic settlement. As more and more Native land was taken for roads, oil wells, and train stations, its population grew. The deer owners who had lost their deer went to live there. The young people, having wandered about the Earth without finding themselves, returned, trying to take hold of the traditional skills of their fathers. But alas! The skills no longer existed. Their roots had been severed forever. It was here that the most shameful trade began, instigated by the intellectuals of the Native people, the elite of the nation, who began to trade away the land of their people—a foot of land for a comfortable house that became a coffin. The trade continued until all the lands were gone, and coffins were built by the hundreds, only to stand empty. Later, however, two or three families crowded into each of these coffins.

The moles came here last, unable to survive on their own, migrating with the few remaining deer. And they were met by mocking jokes and the scornful laughter of the worms, who had their moment of triumph. Like howling evil dogs, the worms greeted the caravans, throwing stones at the deer.

The last of the free people passed through the Horde as if running a gauntlet. Many were killed and mutilated. The rest set up their dwellings for good, in this shameful place of death. The women caressed the deer for the last time. The men held their life-brothers by the mane, fell on their knees, then raised the executioner's ax. They let the ax fall without realizing that their souls were now dead forever.

At that moment a new era began, an era of slavery. For people without labor—labor assigned to their hands, mind, and soul by God—turn into slaves.

Leonty Taragupta (KHANTY)
(

A Khanty poet and folklorist, **Leonty Taragupta** was born in 1945 in the village of Poslovy in the Yamal-Nenets autonomous region. Educated at the Teacher's College of Salekhard and the Chelyabinsk Cultural Institute, he has been recording Khanty folklore since 1975. He is a member of the Academic Institute of the Yugra-Obs people in Salekhard, where he now lives. Taragupta devotes his time to restoring the ancient Khanty Bear Feast epic and native philosophy, as well as restoring the art of making native musical instruments. The song and prayer below were recorded from the Yamal fisherman Peter Yarkin in the early 1980s and translated into Russian by Taragupta and Igor Kravtsov.

In "Son of the Sky" and "The Prayer of the Bear" the son of the master of towns and hamlets is the ancient Khanty hunter who kills the Bear. The Son of the Sky is the Sacred Bear himself, son of *Numi Torum,* the supreme god of the Khanty, Father of the Skies. The forest giants are powerful spirits, malevolent toward men, but often stupid. The White-Neck Mother is the ancient She-Deer. At times the Bear speaks in the first person, and the final lines are from the mouth of *Numi Torum.* Bear worship is known through virtually the whole of Siberia, from the Komi people west of the Ural Mountains to the Ainu of Sakhalin Island.

SON OF THE SKY
(sacred song of the Bear Feast, of the first hunt and origin of the ritual)

Inherited
by the Son
of the mighty Master of Towns,
inherited
by the Son
of the mighty Master of Hamlets,
the antlered deer
covered with sweat
through the long summer
through the gadfly season
were released into the forest
as the World turned
to the time of the autumn hunt.

When the Father of the Seventh Sky
sent sable snow
to the people,
the snow marked
with sable tracks,
the Son of the Master of Towns,
the Son of the Master of Hamlets
remembered his deer,
remembered his herd.
In the ice
he noticed
distant deer tracks.
Coming closer,
he saw other tracks:

the sacred Son of the Sky
in his long-haired coat
had passed here.

The Son of the Master of Towns,
the Son of the Master of Hamlets,
chased him a long time,
following in his tracks.
At last he raised
his eight-layered bow
and took an arrow
from his magic quiver.
His shoulder moved
and the eight-layered bow
resounded through the woods
with the thunder of river-ice in spring.
I was unable to remove
the sharp point of the arrow
entangled in my long-haired coat.
The small sharp point of the arrow
took my sacred heart,
took my taiga heart.
The Son of the Master of Towns,
the Son of the Master of Hamlets,
threw me upon
the sledge behind him
and took me to his wife,
the skillful needle master
in the women's corner
where the firewood is stored.
Into his sable nest
onto his downy seat
he fell like a broad-shouldered pine.

THE PRAYER OF THE BEAR

O Father of the Seven Skies—
I too have been a God-spirit,
descendant of the bright ancestor,
descendant of the all-hearing ancestor,
though set upon the firmament
of the Earth!
But the Son of the Master of Towns—
is he your Father's heir?
the Son of the Master of the Hamlets—
is he your Mother's heir?
O Father of the Seven Skies?
Please send down
ten mighty animals
from the abundant celestial pastures!

And ten mighty animals
did descend.
I hear the Son of the Master of Towns
went into the woods.
Like the crack of the briar nut
on strong teeth
he slew the celestial messengers.
Like the crack of the cherry nut
on strong teeth
he slew the celestial messengers.
And into his sable nest
onto his downy seat
he fell like a broad-shouldered pine.

I too have been a God-spirit.
O Mother, hear me!
O Father, hear me!
Please send down
twenty mighty animals from
the abundant celestial pastures.

As soon as
twenty mighty animals
were set upon the firmament
of the Earth
the piercing cries
of the forest giants
rose again
in the woods near the house.
But they died out again
with a crack of the cherry nut
on the strong teeth
of the Son of the Towns.
They died out again
with a crack of the briar nut
on the strong teeth
of the Son of the Hamlets.
I hear
he fell again
into his sable nest
onto his downy seat
like a broad-shouldered pine tree.

O Father of the Seven Skies,
my forefather, hear me!
O Mother of the Seven Skies,
my foremother, hear me!
The Son of the Master of Towns—

is he your Father's heir?
The Son of the Master of Hamlets—
is he your Mother's heir?
Please send down
the leader of the hundred animals,
my mother the White-Neck!

In the woods by the house
the piercing cries
of the forest giants
rise again.
The Son of the Master of Towns
goes into the woods.
The crack of the cherry nut
on strong teeth
is all I hear.
The crack of the briar nut
on strong teeth
is all I hear.
Yet by the White-Necked Deer
by my White-Neck Mother
by the eight-layered bow
he is brought to the ground.

O Son of the Master of Towns,
O Son of the Master of Hamlets,
you have slaughtered
my offspring,
the mighty animals,
with the crack of a briar nut
on strong teeth—
you have destroyed them
with the crack of a cherry nut
on strong teeth.

But the sacred clan-mother,
the great White-Neck
you cannot destroy!

Now,
since you have overthrown
at daybreak
that poor son of mine
sent from the skies,
you shall spread the
sacred happy news of him
to the towns and the hamlets,
including your own sinful town.
You shall raise
a sacred house
higher than the highest
beautiful houses.
You shall make
a broad flooring of three planks
in the western corner.
You shall encircle
this bright home
with sacred smoke.
You shall humbly rest
the head of the good son
on that fresh flooring
with a bowl of hot food before it
and a bowl of hot food behind.
Only when this is done
at the man-dance
may the children of the three tribes
come together.
Only when this is done
may you hear

the five songs of the taiga
from five open-hearted sons.
And only after this
may you call for the
hump-backed
merry pranksters.
And in the future
when the lovely woman-faced happy world
shall come to pass,
when the hunting tracks
of the blood-children
shall blaze without fear—
children of the eternal tree,
dwellers of the Lower World,
children of the severed navel cord—
you shall remember
my testament.

YURI RYTKHEU (CHUKCHEE)

(

Yuri Rytkheu (1930–2008), a Chukchee writer, was born in the small village of Uelen on the Chukotka Peninsula, the easternmost extremity of the Siberian Russian Arctic. His heritage was that of a coastal big-sea game-hunting and warrior culture. His name—*rit-geu*—which he received from his grandfather, means the Unknown One. Ironically, such anonymity would be reversed during the course of his long career.

After seven years of school, Rytkheu went to live in the neighboring Eskimo village of Naukan to hunt walrus. He worked various odd jobs in the area, finally making his way to the major local city of Anadyr, where he attended the teacher training college. Next he moved to St. Petersburg (then Leningrad) to continue his education. It was there that his writing career began. Rytkheu wrote in both Chukchee and Russian.

All in all, Rytkheu's writing has been prolific yet uneven. On the one hand, he had undertaken a tremendous challenge—to reveal to the general reader the unique world and culture of his people, the Chukchees. For this achievement he was later rightfully declared to be the founder of Chukchee literature, and he himself a living classic. He wrote poetry, fiction (both novels and short stories), essays, and criticism. He also collected folktales, gave many interviews, and received many awards. On the other hand, he expended much energy writing about political matters, making an extensive effort to glorify the coming of the Revolution and the Soviet Power to Chukotka. His first collection of short stories, *Folks from Our Shore* (1953), was written in Chukchee and published in Russian.

As time passed, Rytkheu rarely visited his own people in Chukotka, choosing to live among the cultural elite of Moscow and St. Petersburg, or in Europe, where he lectured and promoted his writings. Working for UNESCO, he became an international icon of Chukchee culture, a world expert on the North.

From time to time Rytkheu was capable of producing good and lasting fiction, especially in his later years, when he began to experiment with traditional mythology in a fictional context. Such were his novellas *When the Whales Go* (1975, filmed in the 1980s), and *Tariky* (1979), both based on ancient Chukchee legends, which he successfully remade into contemporary cross-cultural parables. "Kakot's Numbers," one of the best of Rytkheu's short stories, was first published in 1970 in the Russian magazine *Znamya* (#7). It has been continuously reprinted ever since and remade into a novel, *The Magic Numbers* (1986), perhaps the best among Rytkheu's pieces. Some of his other novels include *Son at the Beginning of the Mist* (1969), *Hoarfrost on the Threshold* (1970), *The End of Permafrost* (1977), and *Aivangu* (1980).

Notwithstanding the cultural and ideological personal conflicts that accompanied him through his career, Rytkheu was a gifted and genuinely Native phenomenon. As he stated in his article "People of the Long Spring" (translated into English for *National Geographic,* February 1983): "Regardless of where fate might cast us up, for us, the return to our native soil is always a return to that point from which we see the world."

KAKOT'S NUMBERS

When Amundsen decided to take Kakot as his cook, the Chukchees came on board the *Maud* to plead with him to change his mind, suggesting he choose another man.

Kakot himself stood aside, keeping silent, his face full of deliberation and suffering. His eyes traced the wandering shoreline of Stoneheart Point, beyond the harbor where the *Maud*, locked in ice, was spending the winter. The mere idea that he would leave this gray ship was unbearable to him.

"You don't want to go?" Amundsen asked him.

Kakot nodded silently.

"I can take someone else," Amundsen said.

Without a word, Kakot started for the gangplank, intending to go ashore.

"Hold on!"

Amundsen rushed toward him, reproaching himself for his sentimentality, but he couldn't help himself. He had taken a sudden sympathy toward this man, so different from his fellow Chukchees, those Arctic optimists who never stopped smiling—even during the dark and hungry months of winter.

Kakot lingered by the gangplank.

"You're on board," Amundsen said loudly, so everyone could hear.

Gottfried Hansen, who stood beside him, grinned into his mustache. Thus Kakot came to live on board the *Maud,* in a small cabin with only a cot and a little table attached to the wooden wall.

During his first day on the job, the new cook was given a steam sauna and cloth trousers, but he kept his own sealskin boots. Amundsen himself taught him how to cook. There was a stove in the kitchen, plus a variety of pots and pans. Beside the stove stood an enormous container in which oatmeal was heated all day long, which the crew would later eat with gusto. Before long, Kakot knew how to roast meat, to make soup and stew, but he never learned how to bake. The big-nosed Amundsen did the baking himself while Kakot stood nearby, watching the Norwegian make magic with the dough, putting the little buns into the oven then taking them out, plump and brown.

In the evenings, after supper, Kakot carefully washed his hands over the tub, scrubbed his face with a bit of wet cloth, then squeezed into the wardroom, where strange spirit-like sounds came from the throat of the gramophone, taking his mind away from places he wished never to see again: the grave of his cherished wife, the place where his little daughter—a spring fledgling, the sunlight of his life—now lived among strangers.

The explorers were happy. They played strange games, writing on sheets of paper. Kakot understood that the signs on those sheets were *words,* written so you could send a message to anyone, or to make a note for the future.

But one man always wrote something different from the others. Oscar Visting. He would take a seat at the end of the big table and open a thick ledger full of small, neat signs. Then he would study them with evident satisfaction, sometimes moving his lips and whispering to himself.

One evening Kakot couldn't contain his curiosity.

"Are those good words?" he asked.

"Where?" Visting started.

"Right there." Kakot pointed at the page, where the strange signs stood in strict columns.

"Those aren't words," Visting replied. "They're numbers."

Visting spoke English, so Kakot understood him. But he didn't yet know the word for *numbers.*

"What?"

"Numbers?" Visting asked pensively. "Why, how can I

explain it . . . ? Here is your finger." He pointed at Kakot's finger, the nail of which had been neatly trimmed by Amundsen himself. "There's a second right beside him, a third, a fourth, and a fifth. So I use the number five to designate five fingers. Is that clear?"

"It'd be easier to draw a hand," Kakot said.

Puzzled, Visting looked at the sad Chukchee.

The sign that Visting used for five fingers strangely excited Kakot, and at times, right in the midst of his work, he would suddenly stop, lost in thought, and stare at his hands, remembering the little figure that looked like a hook for the big kettle, the sign that held inside of it the meaning of five human fingers. His one hand was just like the other; then came his feet, each with as many toes as the fingers on his hands. The entire amount, called *klikkin* by the Chukchee, meant a man, or a person of masculine gender, although the total number for a woman was the same. Still, the number used for counting was *klikkin*. All great numbers were counted in units of twenty.

Big numbers. The coastal dwellers had no real need for them. There were enough fingers and toes to count the walrus or seals they killed, and in better times you could add the hands and feet of family members, which were always visible, for in the warmer part of their dwellings no one wore heavy clothing, and everyone went without boots.

Kakot worked at the stove and contemplated the numbers. Amundsen had made him a big cook's hat and a special apron, a *kamleika*, of white cloth. It was meant to be worn only in the kitchen, but for Kakot and his clansmen such clothing was better designed for hunting the polar fox, or for crawling across the ice toward a seal. One cook's hat and one white apron. But there were three casseroles. Everything in the kitchen could easily be counted.

Every evening Visting would sit at the end of the table and write down his numbers. Judging from these signs, there were unimaginably large numbers, impossible to grasp. How many would that be when counted in twenties? An immensity! Kakot would draw near Visting and, when the latter felt his breath over his ear, he would raise his head. Then the cook, feeling embarrassed, would move away.

Once Visting couldn't help but asking, "Does this interest you?"

"Very much!" Kakot replied, his heart thumping.

So Oscar Visting explained more numbers—one, two, three, and so on, up to ten.

Kakot grasped the general idea, but failed at ten. Not for long, though. On the fifth evening he understood that the Whites, unlike the Chukchees, counted by tens, not twenties.

Thereafter, for everything suited for counting, Kakot wrote down numbers, drawing them so accurately that his written ones looked almost like printed figures. Everything he looked at had to be counted. He counted the members of the crew, the visitors, the polar fox hides that Amundsen used for trade, the hides of the polar bears that hung on the deck. He saved every scrap of paper that others had thrown away, carefully laying them flat, so that in the evening, sitting by Oscar Visting in the wardroom to the sound of the gramophone, he might write down in numbers all that he had seen during the day.

When the scraps of paper were full, Kakot got down on the ice and drew numbers in the snow with an iron poker.

The dogs followed him, for they connected him to the most attractive place on board ship—the kitchen. Carefully they sniffed at the figures in the snow, digging under them, trying to find some delicacy; then, disappointed, they moved aside and looked back at the cook, who was standing on the snow with an amazed and silly expression on his face.

Ashamed of his own behavior, Kakot wrote his numbers alone, or only with Oscar Visting, who stared at him with a derisive smile while wondering, "What does this man find so special about numbers?" To him it was senseless.

"How much is this?" Visting asked him once, pointing at a figure on a Lipton Tea box.

"That's Alexander Kisk and his fourteen dogs," Kakot answered, clearly remembering the trader who had approached the ship, hooked his team to the pole, then come aboard, immediately sniffing the air to detect if there was any vodka around. When Kakot gave him some whortleberry syrup, the trader sniffed it for a long time, tried a bit on his tongue, and then, making a face, gulped it like bitter medicine.

The greater the numbers became for Kakot, the less concrete they appeared, as if they had somehow lost their link to familiar places or events. So he stopped writing them down.

Visting noticed and, thinking the cook was out of paper, gave him a beautiful thick notebook used for recording observations on magnetic phenomena.

For a long time Kakot didn't touch it. Grave forebodings seized him every time he leafed through the empty, virgin-white pages. How many figures one could put in here! What numbers, what unthinkable multitudes these lines could hold! It takes your breath away! And yet everything began with the number one, a little vertical bar, meaning *single*. One man, one fly, one dog, one ship, one Kakot, one Amundsen . . . one daughter! A daughter who lived in a far-off village with distant relatives.

One evening Kakot couldn't stand it any longer. He locked himself in his cabin and opened the notebook. He had a sharp pencil in his hand. And in the upper left-hand corner of the first page he wrote "1"—then stopped. This was his daughter. He dropped the pencil, rested his head on his fist, and the child's face appeared before his eyes.

The next day Kakot told Amundsen he had to take leave.

"What's the matter, Kakot?" Amundsen asked. "Don't you like it here?"

"I like it," the cook replied sadly. "But I must go and visit my daughter. I think that she's ill."

(

When everyone on board the *Maud* had lost all hope of his return, Kakot appeared one day inside the wardroom with something bundled in fur. Inside the deer hides lay his daughter, a girl of six.

As they unwrapped her, even the experienced travelers averted their eyes—the tiny, terribly thin body of the child was nearly covered with scabs.

Amundsen gave a deep sigh, shook his head, and said decisively, "Hot water, soap, and clean towels, please!"

Immediately everyone tried to help. One brought a copper tub, another carried in a huge bucket of warm water, a third offered advice, while Amundsen, rolling up his shirtsleeves and putting on an apron, worked with scissors along the girl's head, cutting away thin strands of hair full of lice.

Only Kakot wasn't busy, sitting alone, outwardly indifferent, as if that wasn't his daughter being bathed in the copper tub.

As he looked at her, he realized that numbers possessed yet another quality—the capacity to diminish. Consider his daughter. This was all that was left of her from the terrible disease that had ravaged his kin—his parents, his wife, his brothers and sisters. Almost all of the village had died out. Those that remained alive could be counted within the limits of one man. *Klikkin.* Just twenty.

Caring for Kakot's daughter inspired the crew of the *Maud.* Within weeks their efforts had turned Mary into a lovely little girl. Kakot often caught himself wondering, "Was this really his daughter?" But her eyes, her facial expression, even the color of her hair served to remind him more and more of his deceased wife.

In the evenings, in the wardroom, Mary listened to the many plans for her future. And when it was finally decided that she, along with the younger daughter of Charles Carpenter, the trader, would be educated in Oslo, Amundsen asked Kakot if he would agree to it. But Kakot had made his decision long ago. He had only one fear—that Amundsen might give it a second thought. What man would deny his daughter a brighter future? Kakot knew only too well that, among white people, even the poorest life could not compare with the constant hunger of the seacoast. Yet he stood to lose his daughter forever. If Mary graduated in far-off Oslo and became a totally different person, would she want to return to her native land? What would she do there, if she couldn't process hides, cut the carcass of a seal, sew sealskin boots, and *kuhlianka* robes for her husband?

Instead, she would know the essence of large numbers.

And so Kakot returned to his figures.

Opening to the first page, he saw the number 1 standing alone in the upper left-hand corner as if looking for guests, for companions. Below it Kakot slowly wrote the figure 2. Then it was 3's turn. Before long he had to begin another column, and the numbers wouldn't stop. It felt like an avalanche had let loose, its noisy flow pouring over the clean pages of the notebook.

Kakot felt hot. Beads of perspiration formed on his forehead, as if he had been carrying the carcass of a fat deer on his back. His breath came faster and faster. The point of his pencil jumped as if alive. Figures flowed from its little pointed end, one after another, forming columns.

Then, with much difficulty, Kakot withdrew his pencil from the page and threw it down. It struck the deck with a dull sound. It took an even greater effort to close the notebook. Even through its thick cover, he could sense the invisible power of those numbers, a mysterious radiation.

He searched about for a hiding place to keep the notebook out of sight, where it wouldn't tempt him with its scores of empty pages, pages just waiting for the invasion of magic numbers. He took a sealskin bag from beneath his cot and put the notebook right on the bottom, under a pair of leather mittens and his extra sealskin boots.

In the evenings to come, he kept away from Oscar Visting

in the wardroom, to avoid falling victim to his large numbers. He played with his daughter, who grew more beautiful each day, adorned with new clothing sewn for her in turn by the members of Roald Amundsen's expedition.

The electric lamp gave a steady light, a far-off melody poured from the gramophone's throat, and the deck above creaked under the thick snow. Time passed peacefully, bringing closer the moment when all would return to their cabins. Conversation dwindled like a lamp low on oil, while Kakot's soul seethed with restlessness.

He sought his cabin reluctantly, opening the thin plank door slowly and entering anxiously. He had just enough strength to resist the sealskin bag under his cot, to avoid being seduced by that ill-fated notebook, the source of all that was mysterious and unknown.

The numbers obsessed him—the way they wanted to make their way onto the white paper. The very spirit of those large, ever-increasing figures touched him feverishly. They stretched on endlessly, overwhelming him in a way that Oscar Visting didn't seem to understand.

The feeling compelled him to study the people on board the *Maud*. Sometimes he didn't hear the words Amundsen spoke to him but just stared at his mouth, at the tip of his rosy tongue, at his big strong teeth and wondered: is this the man, who, as they say, has conquered great distances? Who went so far south there was nowhere left to go? Does he possess the truth of the endlessly growing numbers? Probably not—because Amundsen is always looking for the end, the very edge of the earth, certain that there are limits to the earth and its oceans. But beyond the beasts, the people and plants, beyond all that surrounds man from his birth to his last hour, beyond all that can be counted, beyond the very end itself, numbers exist. An endless line of numbers—the mysterious growth of quantity. Was there an end to that endlessness?

Kakot stood there, holding his tray in his hands, oblivious to what Amundsen was saying.

"Are you deaf?" Amundsen screamed in his ear.

Kakot looked at him compassionately, thinking that this man with the loud voice and formidable appearance was but one of many people. A member of the human family. One human specimen. One could count not only the crew of the *Maud* but people on the opposite coast as well. One could even count the dwellers of far-off Norway, from where Amundsen and his companions had come.

"How many people are there in Norway?" Kakot asked, ignoring Amundsen's angry voice.

"What?" Amundsen was stupefied.

"How many people are there in Norway?" Kakot repeated.

Amundsen stepped back, turned abruptly, and left the narrow kitchen. Kakot could hear his loud voice for a long time after.

Then he retreated to his cabin and quickly packed his few belongings. He was no longer afraid of the notebook with its numbers. He put it on the very top, in order to feel its firm cover through the skin of the rucksack.

Amundsen wouldn't talk to him. He sent Oscar Visting instead, the man who had revealed to Kakot the mystery of numbers, without comprehending himself the mysterious power of their increasing multitudes.

"Roald Amundsen wants to know," Visting said, "if you want to stay on board and work, or go ashore?"

Oscar Visting. Just one member of all the uncountable people on earth.

"Ashore," Kakot answered. "I'm going back to my people."

He went ashore that very evening, carrying on his shoulder a leather trunk that contained the sealskin bag with his notebook, in which he had inscribed the first columns of an endless succession of numbers.

His daughter Mary stayed on board. Where could he take

her? He had no *yaranga,* no home of his own, or even close relatives. The only thing he could do was to seek out someone's *yaranga* as an adopted husband.

Not far from the icy harbor where the *Maud* was wintering, Kakot found shelter with a lonely widow who took a fancy to the precious commodities with which he had been paid for his work—pieces of spotted cloth, three cases of biscuits, two sacks of flour, and a few other items.

As soon as he had settled down, Kakot took out the notebook and went to work. He decided to write down as many numbers as he could stand. He had no sense of guilt—he had brought enough food into the *yaranga* so as not to feel obliged to the woman who now looked upon him as a provider.

At dawn he crawled from the warm part of the dwelling and settled into a colder section, placing the notebook on a low table. Hunting gear hung on the wall in front of him, but he didn't even raise his eyes. Dogs wandered about, looked over his shoulder, tried to lick at the lowered wet forehead, but the man was immersed in his numbers.

Sometimes he would lift eyes from the notebook and stare into space above the dogs lying in the *chottagin,* the half-open *yaranga* door.

His wife would come by, trying not to disturb him. If anybody had asked him at that moment for his first wife's name, he wouldn't have remembered. Tremendous columns of numbers! The whole of humanity was nothing compared to them. Not a single man. Not even Amundsen himself!

Sometimes neighbors would peer into the *yaranga,* watching Kakot from a distance, as if he was stricken with some contagious disease. He didn't feel the need for communication. What would they talk about? He had already lost all interest in talk of the currents, the condition of the ice, the seals that, with the coming of spring, were starting to come out on the ice more often. And his new wife understood him. She didn't say a word.

Quite the opposite: she tried to protect him from the intrusion of the more curious visitors.

She sensed somehow that her new partner was troubled with something very important, something inaccessible not only to her but their neighbors.

And so Kakot continued recording his numbers, unable to pronounce the greatest figure on the page of his notebook, a number that reason itself couldn't fathom!

And yet one could add just one more number to it and get a new result, then another and another, continuing for days . . .

In the evenings Kakot was so exhausted that he didn't pay attention to the tasty meals his wife cooked for him, having bartered for delicacies with his flour and biscuits.

When the lamp went out, Kakot would feel the passionate caresses of the woman who craved the kind of attention she had missed for so long. But he responded without enthusiasm, thinking only that if they were lucky enough to conceive a child, it would balance the sum total of mankind, as it was most likely that someone was dying right then, and thus the total number of people would remain roughly the same. But even if humanity grew in number, it wasn't infinite.

Once, at an opportune moment, Kakot's wife stole a look at his notebook, but she was unable to comprehend anything about the long columns of figures. The signs were unlike anything she'd ever seen. Definitely there was something in them, because Kakot sat absorbed by them, even groaning now and then from his efforts.

She held the notebook close to her face, trying to breathe in something unknown, then felt a scrutinizing gaze on her. Turning around, she met the deep black eyes of Kakot. He wasn't angry; he was looking at her with interest and expectation.

But from the eyes of his woman Kakot could tell that, unlike himself, she felt nothing toward the numbers, nothing she could express in words.

Kakot took the notebook and opened to the page where he had stopped writing. And as he looked into the long columns of numbers, the excitement, so well known to him, returned. Strange wings lifted him, carrying him away into a world of pure thought, while his wife retreated behind a fur screen.

Spring came and melted the ice along the coast. Birds flew back north toward the watery expanses now opened to them. And the Norwegians came after Kakot, to ask if he'd like to say good-bye to his daughter.

Kakot got on his sledge and went, taking his notebook with him.

He soon found before him a girl totally different from the one he'd left behind. *Him.* She was already able to pronounce some Norwegian words, and she looked at her father with amazement, even tried to keep her distance, touching his shaggy beard tentatively, so different from the thick dense hair of the Norwegians.

Kakot tried to imagine how difficult it would be for her in the *yaranga*—the walls stained with smoke, the smell of oil lamps, the slimy dampness behind the cold, fur screen—and felt happy that she was going to a better country.

That evening in the wardroom he sat down by Oscar Visting and, with an air of importance, opened his notebook. Looking over his shoulder, Visting whistled in amazement.

He took the notebook from Kakot and went to show it to the other crew members. Amundsen himself picked it up, leafing through it page by page for a long time, uttering some very strange words; but since they had nothing to do with cooking, Kakot didn't understand them.

Yet he sensed that even these white men couldn't grasp the concept of infinity. It wasn't a matter of adding numbers one by one. It was something impossible to express. Ultimately, it meant the denial of the meaning of life, the absence of any goal. Such an idea wasn't for human beings to experience. To do so would only acknowledge the hopelessness of the human condition.

But the Norwegian explorers soon forgot about Kakot's notebook, intent on completing their mission—the Northwest Passage! Some, having crossed the polar seas, were actually finishing a voyage around the world.

Kakot closed his notebook carefully and went out on the deck unnoticed. From there he went down to the ice and made his way ashore. It was a bright night. The sun stood on the very horizon. In weather like this it was easy to walk home to your village.

And so he went into the bright misty night, leaving the *Maud* behind him with his daughter aboard. She would go to far-off lands and never know cold or hunger, two ever-present facts of Chukchee life.

Ice creaked beneath his feet, and his breath filled the silence of the frigid coast. Thoughts rushed from his head, forming voices around him. This was the way he had taken a year ago in the spring, struggling through the sun-polished ice cliffs. He had gone to see the famous Akre, the master of Arakamchechen Island, a powerful and friendly shaman, whom he had hoped could save his wife.

The shaman had listened to his sad story in silence, and his reply brought Kakot to a strange acceptance of his fate.

"Do not grieve much, my lad," the shaman had said. "Nothing can help your wife now. She has gone beyond the clouds, like so many before her. There is nothing you or I can do about it. That's how life is. It's not for us to try to change it. Grief is part of life, just like joy. . . ."

The shaman spoke for a long time, convincingly, but Kakot had seen before him only his wife's dying eyes, had heard only the loud cry of his hungry daughter. She had been hungry from the moment she was born. Her first word, something only a parent could understand, had sent a clear message. It meant to eat.

Had man been created solely to live out his years searching for food and a warm corner for shelter?

When the night was almost over, with the sun already high above the expanse of the sea, Kakot sat down for a minute on a melted ice shelf, looking behind him for the first time. All of a sudden he felt a strange and gnawing pain inside, as if someone had torn away a piece of his flesh, leaving the wound open. Only now did he realize that his daughter had remained on the boat—his daughter, the sole extension of his life, his only reminder of the loved one who had gone beyond the clouds.

Turning immediately, Kakot ran back along the coast, jumping over the melting ice floes.

But the *Maud* had sailed far from shore, avoiding the nearby points of land. No crew member heard the scream that came from the very depths of Kakot's heart. Growing weaker, the tormented cry died down, to be lost in the great cold silence of the sea.

Kakot lowered his head and returned to the village sadly. He took out his notebook again, but now it required a great effort for him to record his figures. He felt as if he were working against his heart's desire.

Before long he began hunting again, going to sea, bringing game into his *yaranga*. It was easy to get seals in springtime, which made his woman happy—her husband had become a real provider.

In her caresses Kakot felt something new now, which made him think. And from these thoughts came a deeper longing for his daughter. With great clarity he understood how stupid and cruel it was to have put her into the hands of Roald Amundsen. Why had he done so? His daughter hadn't lived with him for very long. When his wife was alive, she had taken care of Mary, and after her death their relatives had taken her in.

Something was happening with the numbers now. No matter how fast he tried to write them, their end would recede just as fast. And where *was* that end? Infinity, he realized, was beyond definition!

When the sea grew free of ice, boats went out to hunt walrus, and Kakot joined one of the teams. He worked hard as a harpooner and earned his share of the spoils, spending his evenings sitting beside the *chottagin* and writing numbers—until the passionate sighs of his woman pierced the warm fur screen.

The numbers began to fill the second half of his notebook. Each time he sat down on a piece of whalebone, Kakot expected a miracle to happen. He hoped the numbers would take on a new dimension, reveal some obscure meaning behind the silent columns of enormous sums.

But the numbers were silent.

Their essence would not reveal itself. To the average man, this notebook was just a simple set of ever-increasing numbers. But for Kakot, its pages seemed to contain his entire life, all of his deliberations on the essence of things. How could anyone else discern among the hills of icy figures the longing for the daughter that Amundsen had taken away?

Summer flew by unnoticed. Kakot covered his *yaranga* with new walrus skins, filled the wooden barrels with walrus fat, and repaired the fur screen within. Yet his main concern was still the notebook, in which the columns of numbers were now approaching the last page.

Then Kakot grew worried. He suddenly saw signs that he was losing his connection to other people. The realization came to him when he noticed the big belly of his wife. Life was going on about him while he worked at his numbers. The future was coming, irrespective of his painful deliberations.

He tried to be tender to his wife, to talk to her, but often caught himself falling silent in the middle of his own words, only to return to his cherished notebook.

Snow fell from the sky. The sea was covered with ice again, and the bloody trails of slain seals led to the *yarangas*.

Kakot left early in the morning and returned by starlight. He lit a bright lamp and hung it by the door.

Ice closed in on the village. There would be no more open water until spring. The watery route by which his daughter had left lay entirely frozen.

One day Kakot returned to the place where the *Maud* had wintered. There were no signs that the ship of the famous explorer had even been there. The sea, lined with icy cliffs, spread away for immense distances too vast for the eye, yet one could mentally trace the route of the *Maud* its entire way home. The ship was headed for Nome, and Kakot had been to Nome— nothing but a cluster of small wooden houses. And where was Norway, and the city of Oslo?

Something pierced Kakot's heart. He had suddenly realized that he couldn't imagine where Olso was, or Norway itself, the land for which his daughter had sailed. His daughter, to whom he had given the foreign name of Mary. Perhaps the problem wasn't in the numbers but in himself. Was he to blame for his wife's death—he hadn't taken care of her—and for the abominable thing he had done in agreeing to give his daughter to Roald Amundsen?

Yes, the explorer had said she would return when she learned how to speak and write. But a literate Mary would not be Kakot's daughter!

Back in the village, his wife awaited him.

Not just his wife but a person with a name—*Veamneut*. River Woman. At this very moment she might be giving birth, while he brooded and wandered on the ice, looking for the significance of impossibly large numbers.

Kakot headed for the coast, returning without a catch, having spent his time in calculations and memories. He shouldn't have gone. Memories had stirred his soul, bringing back thoughts that made him sweat with fear. His notebook lay inside the sealskin bag on his back, its weight a constant reminder of the importance of large numbers.

Now the numbers burned through his white *kamleika* robe, pierced his fur *kuhlianka* coat, squeezing his tormented heart. Confused thoughts rushed into his head, his blood beating at his temples.

He stopped to catch his breath, automatically removing the sealskin bag from his pack. Unthinkingly, he unfastened its thongs and took out the notebook. It looked swollen because of the immense numbers inside—if not from the numbers themselves then from the dampness, the inevitable drops of fat from the oil lamp.

Without opening it, Kakot set the notebook in the snow and stepped aside. A few more steps and it would be out of sight. Then the wind would tear it away, page by page.

But suppose someone found these strange pages and started thinking? He might abandon his hunter's walking stick and forget what he had gone onto the ice for—to hunt seals—fixing his eyes instead on the curious sign.

Returning to the swollen notebook, Kakot squatted beside it. It was breathing. Such a terrible sight! Buffeted by the wind, it seemed alive.

He poked it with his walking stick, and the pages ruffled in the wind, the black rows of numbers dancing before him, as if leaping into the snow.

"I must destroy it," he decided. Setting his rifle aside, he sat down on his skis and removed a leather pouch from his coat. There was a matchbox within, covered with tobacco crumbs. He blew them away, took out a match, and lit it. The paper's edge blackened, then burst into a bright yellow flame.

It was strange. Although the pages burned quickly, the numbers themselves seemed to remain, resisting the fire, as if reluctant to disappear.

Page by page Kakot burned the ill-fated notebook. The little fire burned brightly, then faintly, licking at the black columns of numbers.

Then the last page turned in the wind, burning along with the cover, and Kakot stirred the fire so it wouldn't go out.

When the last scrap was gone, only a small heap of gray ashes remained. Kakot nudged it with the edge of his boot and the ashes scattered, leaving a small depression in the snow.

He sighed deeply and looked about.

The ice cliffs were closing in on him. Night was coming. Countless stars filled the sky. But there was no need to think of how many there were. It was just a starry sky. A sky full of stars. Just stars in the sky.

Kakot retrieved his hunting gear and started for the village, making his way along the cliffs with the sharp edge of his walking stick.

From a distance he saw the light of his *yaranga* and hastened his pace. In his mind's eye he could see his wife sitting by the low table, carefully supporting her big belly with her knees, waiting for her husband. Half-empty barrels stood outside the walls. Soot blackened the poles and the kettle-chain over the fire. The dogs raised their tired heads and regarded their returning master with indifference.

Simple thoughts, simple ways.

Perhaps, that was the real meaning of life.

Stopping at the door, Kakot saw his wife beside the fur screen within, exactly as he had imagined her, and said aloud: "I'm back! It's me! Kakot!"

Evenk Invocation for Good Fortune

TO NATURE, WHEN THE GREEN RECEDES

(

Dear Mother, your golden ears have heard my words resound like the cawing of the crows. You have seen me from beneath your dense brows. Don't worry, dear Mother. Please don't think that I've come with bad news. Your little children, the birds, who have found refuge on your warm bosom, depart now happy, for you have heard our words and fed us the entire summer, and set before us the bounty of your golden table.

A note on Translation

(

Claude Clayton Smith

Alexander Vaschenko once told a reporter that contemporary Siberia represents a "Wild East" similar to America's "Wild West." Archaeologists and Native American scholars have long believed that the "Indians" migrated to North America from Siberian regions, across a land bridge through the Bering Strait to Alaska; settlement by way of sea travel has been posited as well, from both the Atlantic and Pacific Oceans. Today, Native peoples of this vast region find their way of life threatened by oil spills, industrial pollution, and forest fires, even as the collapse of the former Soviet Union opens new and exciting opportunities to explore this area.

Dr. Vaschenko is the Russian authority on Native American literature and folklore, and he actively promotes research dedicated to the preservation of Native Siberian and Native American culture. He has traveled frequently to Siberia, including visits there with noted Native American author N. Scott Momaday.

The spoken English of Alexander Vaschenko, who has taught in the United States and Canada, is impeccable. Translating hundreds of pages from Russian into English under time constraints, however, was often difficult for him, despite his outstanding language skills and familiarity with Native culture. As I reviewed his translations, polishing his words and adapting them for an English-speaking audience, I discovered a variety of issues inherent in such an undertaking.

First, for example, was the grammatical variation between

the two languages. Here are the opening lines to Yeremei Aipin's reminiscence "Old Man Moon" exactly as I received them from Dr. Vaschenko under the title "Old Man-the-Moon":

> Copper-red face of the Moon was slowly floating out of the pines. Everything: the spring snows, the evening clouds, the houses and the people—have got the same purple red color of the rising moon. When I first saw the enormous round face of the moon, I asked my mother:
> —Who is this over there?
> My mother answered:
> —This is Old Man the Moon.
> Stunned by its vivid complexion and the flaming enormity, I have pointed my finger to it. Mother rebuked me strictly:
> —You should not point your finger to the Old Man.
> —Why? I asked.
> —Your finger will ache. It is a well-known belief, she explained. And, turning to the Old Man, added: "He doesn't like others to point at him. Who would?"

Aside from the punctuation irregularities and general awkwardness, note the verb usage, especially the phrase "I have pointed my finger to it." Russian verb forms distinguish between ongoing action (in the present) and completed action (in the past), while English employs an array of helping verbs to express differences such as "I go," "I am going," "I went," "I have gone," "I had gone," subtleties expressed in Russian by other means. While this presents no great problem in this particular passage, in some narratives I often had trouble following the simple timeline of events, especially in Yuri Rytkheu's short story "Kakot's Numbers," which employs several flashbacks.

Another kind of challenge occurred with Russian words in the text. Rather than distract the reader with footnotes, we incorporated explanations of key terms at the point where they occur. In some cases when translations were unavailable, I made no attempt to find English equivalents. In Yuri Vaella's marvelous short poem "Song of the Reindeer Breeder," the exclamation *Nga-die!* is repeated several times. When I first read the translation, I had no idea what this meant, but it certainly worked in context. Only while preparing the final manuscript did I learn from Dr. Vaschenko that *Nga-die!* is a Nenets exclamation meaning "So be it!" Compare, too, the repeated exclamation *Chovie-chovie!* from Aipin's account of the Bear Feast in chapter 21 of *Morning Twilight* or the myth *Kyingem-Yeingem* in the same chapter. Those words are old and untranslatable and, left as they are, contribute an ancient tone entirely appropriate to the text.

In other instances where the words were indeed translatable, they often resulted in a phrase that begged for improvement when the obvious word choice created a clash of associations. In Aipin's introduction to *Morning Twilight,* the text I received from Dr. Vaschenko mentioned the "Upward-Gone-Man." In my early drafts I retained this literal description, which of course brings to mind Jesus Christ. There are other Christian references in this piece, but it wasn't until I encountered similar parallels in Galina Keptuke's novella *On the Banks of the Jeltula* (see "A Discovery" and "The Unexpected Guest") that I changed Aipin's phrase "Upward-Gone-Man" to the "Risen Man," to emphasize the Christian associations.

The title of Aipin's novel also illustrates an aspect of translation. The novel was originally called *Khanty; or, The Morning Star,* but when Aipin visited me at Ohio Northern University with Dr. Vaschenko in 1996, we changed the title to *Morning Twilight: A Novel of the Khanty.* The change represents a felicitous distinction as well as a happy accident. In English *twilight* means dusk, but the Russian language distinguishes between morning twilight and evening twilight (*zarya* is dawn and *sumerki* is dusk). The happy accident is that *mourning* is a homonym for *morning*, contributing an ironic twist to a novel that mourns the twilight of Khanty culture.

A unique complication arose with Aipin's riddles, one of which I decided to omit because I simply couldn't understand the answer. It read as follows:

O puzzle of mine, puzzle of mine!
Over the mossy log,
over the grassy log,
two sisters
squint at each other
yet can't see each other.
What is it?

The answer is a log. When I asked Dr. Vaschenko to explain, he wrote, "The log is the nose and the two sisters are the eyes." I still didn't get it, so I omitted it. With each of the puzzles, I chose to retain the rather awkward syntax of the opening line, "O puzzle of mine, puzzle of mine!" How else could that read? "I have a riddle. Can you guess the answer?" is too prosaic and lacks the excitement of the exclamation point. I like the difference between *riddle* and *puzzle,* for what are riddles if not puzzling?

In the early 1990s, the poet W. D. Snodgrass and I discussed the translation of poetry. He was then translating the work of a foreign poet, and I was surprised to learn that he and other noted poets use translation as a springboard to riff on the writing of other poets. I was just beginning to review Dr. Vaschenko's translations of Aipin, and I was striving to stay as close as possible to the literal meaning of the original text. Snodgrass gave me the courage to loosen up, especially when I had difficulty making sense of a passage. Although my approach to translation became more flexible, I retained the original imagery and repetitions in most of the poetry in *The Way of Kinship* rather than attempt to rework them for a Western eye and ear.

We are proud to offer to the world this English-language collection of Siberian literature. Mindful of the prehistoric land bridge and those who crossed it, we hope this anthology will become an educational bridge between Native Siberian and Native American cultures, as well as an inspiration to Native storytellers of the future.

ACKNOWLEDGMENTS

(

This book is the culmination of twenty years of collaboration between its editors, a personal and professional association that began with mutual respect for the late Aurelius Piper, Chief Big Eagle of Connecticut's Paugussett Indians, whose dream to create a dialogue between Native Americans and Native Siberians, set in motion with his visits to Russia in 1990 and 1991, has at last been fulfilled.

The editors are grateful to the Mobil Oil Corporation for funding this project in its early stages and to Exxon–Mobil for continuing that funding. At Ohio Northern University, DeBow Freed and Kendall Baker, successive presidents; along with Anne Lippert, vice president for academic affairs; Byron Hawbecker, dean of the College of Arts and Sciences; and English department chairs Eleanor Green, Thomas Banks, and Eva McManus provided sustained and enthusiastic interest, program support, and travel grants. Russian speakers Khristo Boyadzhiev and James Walter assisted with problems in translation, and professors Judy Greavu, Bruce Chesser, and Britt Rowe mounted exhibits of related artwork. Professors Paul Logsdon and Charles Steele provided research assistance and facilitated displays of Native Siberian materials at Heterick Memorial Library. Mike Lackey of the *Lima News* covered many aspects of the project in his columns. Stewart Graham of the Ohio Northern University print shop facilitated the publication of some work in this text in a 1995 chapbook, *I Listen to the Earth,* and Robert Lewis, editor of the *North Dakota Quarterly,* devoted an entire issue to an interim anthology in 2003.

Noted Native American author N. Scott Momaday, walking the path of Chief Big Eagle, wrote the foreword to this volume after visiting with some of its contributors in Siberia. Harry J. Wilson, geographer, designed the map in the frontispiece, in consultation with Susan Scarberry-García, visiting English department scholar at the University of New Mexico. Andrew Wiget, professor of English at New Mexico State University and director of the New Mexico Heritage Center, provided the list of further reading.

To everyone who helped make this text possible, we offer our sincere thanks, concluding with a special thank-you to Charles "Tod" Oliver, Ohio Northern University emeritus professor of English, who introduced the principal editors to each other in the fall of 1989, and to our wives, Marina and Elaine, who endured our absences while we traveled abroad and hosted our foreign colleagues when we were at home.

SUGGESTIONS FOR FURTHER READING

(

For readers who would like to learn more about the history and Native peoples of Siberia, a number of good books in English have become available in the past twenty years. A popular history of the region is *East of the Sun: The Epic Conquest and Tragic History of Siberia* by Benson Bobrick (New York: Henry Holt, 1993). Two books are essential reading: James Forsyth's *A History of the Peoples of Siberia: Russia's North Asian Colony, 1581–1990* (Cambridge: Cambridge University Press, 1992) gives the historical overview indicated by its title, and Yuri Slezkine's *Arctic Mirrors: Russia and the Small Peoples of the North* (Ithaca, N.Y.: Cornell University Press, 1996) details the development of Russian attitudes and policies toward Siberian tribal peoples over the past four centuries, many of which paralleled Anglo-American perspectives on Native Americans. Another useful point of entry is John Ziker's *Peoples of the Tundra: Northern Siberians in the Post-Communist Transition* (Prospect Heights, Ill.: Waveland Press, 2002).

Important perspectives on contemporary Native Siberian attitudes toward their own cultural traditions and the role of Native intellectuals, writers, and politicians in shaping those attitudes are found in the late A. I. Pika's *Neotraditionalism in the Russian North: Indigenous Peoples and the Legacy of Perestroika* (Seattle: University of Washington Press, 1999) and in Patty A. Gray's *The Predicament of Chukotka's Indigenous Movement: Post-Soviet Activism in the Russian Far North* (Cambridge: Cambridge University Press, 2003). More specialized questions are addressed in N. V. Ssorin-Chaikov's *The Social Life of the State in Subarctic Siberia* (Stanford, Calif.: Stanford University Press, 2003).

Until 1990, the standard reference work for Siberian peoples was the English translation of M. G. Levin and L. P. Potapov's book *The Peoples of Siberia* (Chicago: University of Chicago Press, 1956), which still provides valuable information on these peoples, though framed in the Soviet rhetoric of materialist progress obligatory at the time. Beginning in the 1990s, Western anthropologists were able to work in Russia, resulting in several good English-language descriptions of the Native peoples of Siberia, some of whom are represented by the writers in this book.

KHANTY

Balzer, Marjorie. *The Tenacity of Ethnicity: A Siberian Saga in Global Perspective.* Princeton, N.J.: Princeton University Press, 1999.

Jordan, Peter. *Material Culture and Sacred Landscape: The Anthropology of the Siberian Khanty.* Walnut Creek, Calif.: AltaMira, 2003.

NENETS

Golovnev, Andrei, and Gail Osherenko. *Siberian Survival: The Nenets and Their Story.* Ithaca, N.Y.: Cornell University Press, 1999.

NIVKH

Grant, Bruce. *In the Soviet House of Culture: A Century of Perestroikas.* Princeton, N.J.: Princeton University Press, 1995.

EVENK

Anderson, David G. *Identity and Ecology in Arctic Siberia: The Number One Reindeer Brigade.* New York: Oxford University Press, 2002.

Fondahl, Gail. *Gaining Ground? Evenkis, Land, and Reform in Southeastern Siberia.* Boston: Allyn and Bacon, 1997.

Vitebsky, Piers. *The Reindeer People: Living with Animals and Spirits in Siberia*. Boston: Mariner Books, 2006.

CHUKCHEE AND YUPIK

Kerttula, Anna. *Antler on the Sea: The Yupik and Chukchi of the Russian Far East*. Ithaca, N.J.: Cornell University Press, 2000.

Van Deusen, Kira. *Raven and the Rock: Storytelling in Chukotka*. Seattle: University of Washington Press, 1999.

Readers are also directed to the English-language Web site of RAIPON, the Russian Association of the Indigenous Peoples of the North: http://www.raipon.info/en/. The Arctic Council maintains a Web site for affiliated organizations of Arctic Peoples, http://www.arcticpeoples.org.

The Russian authority on Native American literature, **Alexander Vaschenko** is chair of comparative studies in literature and culture at Moscow State University. He is the author of *America against America, Ethnic Literatures of the United States, Historical Epic Folklore of the North American Indians,* and *The Judgment of Paris* (all written in Russian) and editor of *"I Stand in Good Relation to the Earth."*

Claude Clayton Smith is professor emeritus of English at Ohio Northern University. He is the author of *Ohio Outback, Lapping America, Red Men in Red Square, Quarter-Acre of Heartache, The Stratford Devil, The Cow and the Elephant,* and *The Gull That Lost the Sea.*

N. Scott Momaday is a Native American (Kiowa) writer. His novel *House Made of Dawn* was awarded the Pulitzer Prize for Fiction in 1969, and he received the National Medal of Arts in 2007. From 2007 to 2009, he served as poet laureate of Oklahoma. He operates the Buffalo Trust, a nonprofit organization that preserves Native cultures.